One Earth | Three Worlds

T0294079

One Earth | Three Worlds

The Pattern that Connects Dreams, Synchronicity,
Physics, Homeopathy, Spirituality and Somatics

Julian Carlyon

Published in this first edition in 2022 by:
Triarchy Press
Axminster, UK

www.triarchypress.net

ISBNs:
Print: 978-1-913743-65-9
ePub: 978-1-913743-66-6
pdf: 978-1-913743-67-3

tp

for
Julia
my mother
(1924-2007)

Contents

Images and Diagrams

Chapter 7

Fig.1a. Platonic Solids: Drummyfish, CC0, via Wikimedia Commons

Fig.1b. Platonic solids spherical: Based on original from www.cosmic-core.org

Fig.2a. Sphere monochrome: Darkdadaah, CC BY-SA 3.0, via Wikimedia Commons

Fig.2b. Spherical Triangle: Darkdadaah (as above)

Chapter 8

Yin Yang: Klem, Public domain, via Wikimedia Commons

Hexagram 1: Ben Finney, Public domain, via Wikimedia Commons

Hexagram 2: Ben Finney (as above)

Hexagram 34: Ben Finney (as above)

Chapter 12

Simple Vesica Piscis: AnonMoos, Public domain, via Wikimedia Commons

Vesica Piscis circles shaded: Tomruen, CC BY-SA 4.0, via Wikimedia Commons

Christ in Vesica (Codex Bruchsal): Medieval, Public domain, via Wikimedia Commons

Chapter 17

Fig.1. Paul Signac, The Pine Tree at St Tropez, 1909: Public domain, via Wikimedia Commons

Fig.2. Jung/Pauli map: C.G. Jung, 1960/2010, *Synchronicity: An acausal connecting principle*, p.98, Princeton University Press

Cover image

Flammarion Woodcut 1880 Color 2.jpg

Anonymous, Unknown Author via Wikimedia Commons

Introduction

How to introduce this book, so as to give you some idea of what's inside? The first question might be, what kind of book are you looking at? How would I categorise it?

Is it science, spirituality, art, or indeed none or all of these? Well, it draws on science, but I make no claim for it being a scientific explanation for how things are. In fact I suspect that many scientists would dismiss what I have to say as, at best, pseudoscience. There is spirituality in it in as much as I attempt to give central space to the spiritual perception of reality (especially non-dual reality) described throughout the centuries by mystics of both East and West. In the book I will sometimes refer to this spiritual reality as the oneness world, and to spacetime reality – the reality investigated and mapped by modern science – as the twoness world.

Then there's the domain lying, as it were, between the world of modern science and a spiritual understanding of the world, which I've termed the intermediary world. It's the world of the shaman, the healer, the artist and of the psyche, especially the unconscious psyche. It's also the world of scientifically inexplicable connections and events such as telepathy and precognition. It's the world of the bridge between this spacetime reality and the timeless world beyond. It's the world of ritual and those that travel as guides, healers and intermediaries between this world and that world, between time and timelessness. Attempts to investigate this intermediary world are frequently dismissed by scientists, even though an unanswered riddle concerning inexplicable connections lies at the heart of the modern scientific description of nature – namely the enigma of quantum entanglement.

So this book, as well as drawing on science and spirituality, takes an exploratory approach, perhaps more characteristic of art. In other words, I didn't set out with a goal in mind. I set out to follow certain threads – entanglement, synchronicity, consciousness and healing, amongst others – to see where the threads led, and if or how those threads might relate to each other. Rather than knowing where I was going I tried to follow where logic and intuition led me. So I'll call it art, which holds hands with science on one side and spirituality on the other.

That said, here's a little of what to expect.

I take a particular pathway in my attempt to open up a threefold view of reality. I use different ideas and models concerning the nature of things – some well proven, others not – which seem to me consistent with one another and which, taken together, present a coherent view of how things might be. So what are the stepping stones used to make the crossing to this more comprehensive understanding?

I start with physics because it represents a body of knowledge that is well tested against the facts of physical life. I try to get a foothold in the incredibly esoteric world of modern physics. Starting with the foundations laid by Newton and Einstein, I move to the world of uncertainty described by quantum mechanics. My destination here is the theory of quantum entanglement.

With the advent of quantum mechanics in the 1920s the notion of an objective reality operating entirely independently of a human observer was undermined. It was shown that at the level of the very small – photons and electrons – the presence of investigating equipment affects the outcomes of investigation. It was also shown that at the sub-atomic level the position and momentum of a particle cannot be known simultaneously. If you know one you cannot be certain of the other. This uncertainty principle has become enshrined as a law of physics. But quantum mechanics has gone even further. It has shown that at the scale of the very small, events separated in space can be shown to be correlated, to be obviously connected, in the absence of any known causal mechanism relating the two events. The theory of quantum entanglement seems to demonstrate events impossible to understand from the perspective of the already established and proven scientific understanding of forces and causal relationships.

The discussion of quantum entanglement leads easily, and perhaps naturally, to C. G. Jung's theory of synchronicity – *an acausal connecting principle*. Jung was fascinated by the inexplicable occurrences he sometimes witnessed in his practice for which science could provide no satisfactory answers. Can events, objects or people be in a relationship of influence with one another – an influence that might produce demonstrable effects – despite the absence of any demonstrable cause-and-effect link? There are many examples of such influences, some of which I discuss.

From there I introduce the concept of similarity – how things that are similar in nature might be connected to each other in a way that defies normal scientific understanding. My inquiry into similarity leads me on to biologist Rupert Sheldrake's work on morphic resonance and physicist David Bohm's proposed model of an implicate and explicate order.

I include a chapter on homeopathy, a medical system with a long history, supported by a great deal of anecdotal evidence, as well as some robust trials, but which is nevertheless dismissed by the scientific establishment as being nothing more than placebo based on delusional propositions. However, if homeopathy works, then the general hypothesis presented in these pages could point to a reality that displays apparently impossible connections and relationships, which may in some sense be imaginal and yet very real at the same time.

I also look at healing, dreams, creativity, choice and the body from the perspective of the oneness, twoness and intermediary worlds. I then consider spiritual understandings found in the Buddhist tradition, the Christian tradition, and in the classic text of ancient Chinese wisdom, the *I Ching*, to see if the notion of a oneness world, twoness world and intermediary world could make sense from those perspectives. In the final chapter I return again to science and ask what a truly holistic science rooted in these three approaches to reality might look like.

What I offer is not so much a theory as a set of threads which, when woven together, could lead to a more coherent and embracing view of reality and of ourselves.

Julian Carlyon
Stroud, Gloucestershire, UK
May 2022

1. Newton and Einstein

I start this inquiry into the *oneness world, twoness world* and *intermediary world* from the perspective of physics. This seems a good idea in the sense that I can start from fact; that is from scientific hypotheses that have been posited and subsequently proven, or at least not disproven. However I am also cautious about this approach because the world of modern physics is esoteric and difficult to understand. The mathematical equations are way beyond most of us. There can also be different and sometimes conflicting interpretations of the scientific data. For example, the facts of quantum entanglement, which I come to later, are explained using very different interpretations and models. After a hundred years of quantum mechanics there is still wide disagreement about how and why quantum entanglement happens. But, all things considered, I still think it is useful to draw on some of the conclusions of modern physics as a basis and beginning, even though I'll go beyond physics and try and relate to our actual human experience.

I also want to let the reasons for naming these worlds oneness, twoness and intermediary become clearer as we proceed, rather than trying to define them at the outset.

So let's jump in. In the 17th century Isaac Newton established the laws of classical physics. Through the study of bodies in motion he was able to articulate the laws of motion and universal gravitation. He described the mathematical laws governing the motion of objects in space, the effect of forces acting on objects, the law of action and reaction (reciprocal), and the laws governing gravitational attraction.

In the early 20th century Albert Einstein, through his theories of general relativity and special relativity, began the radical shake-up of the observations and theoretical framework of classical physics (classical mechanics).

What was the radical change that occurred between Newton's model of physical reality and Einstein's?

We all know the apocryphal story of Newton and the apple. In a stroke of genius he realised that any massive object exerts an attractive force on other massive objects. This force, for Newton, was the force of gravity. The theory of gravity describes our experience of the motion of physical objects. Gravitational attraction happens between objects of any scale (although, as we shall see, laws that account for the motion of larger objects don't apply in the same way in the world of the very small, the quantum world of electrons and photons). The gravitational force between large objects such as the sun and the earth, or the earth and the moon, or the earth and an apple, is readily apparent (apples fall!). It also exists between an apple and another apple but is so tiny, compared to the pull of the earth on both apples, as to be negligible.

Newton, although he established the equations allowing us to calculate the effect of this force, couldn't explain it and thought it constituted an instantaneous connection between objects (we now know that gravitational waves travel at the speed of light).

In Newton's classical mechanics an object travels through space in a straight line until a gravitational force (from another object) causes it to deviate. Time is treated as a universal constant with a constant rate of passage, independent of the state of motion of an observer.

At the beginning of the 20th century the young and unqualified Albert Einstein was giving this all a lot of thought. He would become one of the century's most celebrated figures. Perhaps the first science superstar!

His thought experiments led to his theory of general relativity. Like all such theories it makes predictions about the behaviour of the physical world. Einstein's theories have been extraordinarily accurate in their predictions. For example, Einstein showed that the universe must be expanding. This prediction was subsequently proved when it was observed that galaxies are indeed accelerating away from each other. This observation helped provide evidence for the big bang theory as the dominant theory of the origin of the universe.

I'll try and summarise Einstein's extraordinary new vision of physical reality – which, however, couldn't and still can't predict or account for events at the quantum level – the world of electrons, photons and so on.

Einstein realised that massive objects such as a planet must distort spacetime. What does this mean? In this view space and time are not separate. Rather space and time form one entity, spacetime. Spacetime is a kind of matrix. It is distorted by massive objects. It curves around an object.

Faraday and Maxwell had already discovered the electromagnetic field through which electromagnetic waves such as radio and light waves are propagated. Einstein realised that gravity must also be a field. Thus the gravitational field and space are one and the same thing. "The gravitational field is not diffused through space; the gravitational field is that space itself."[1] The gravitational field is distorted by massive objects. "Planets circle round the sun, and things fall, because space curves."[2] It was predicted that gravitational waves must therefore exist and they were first observed in 2015.

What other predictions does general relativity make, besides the curvature of space around an object such as the sun? Well, because light passes through the gravitational field, the field must bend light too. This has been proven to be the case.

These observations mark important departures from classical mechanics. Because the gravitational field bends around massive objects, time also gets bent or distorted. Thus "Einstein predicted that time passes more quickly high up than below, nearer to the earth. This was measured and turned out to be the case. If a man who has lived at sea level meets up with his twin who lived in the mountains, he will find that his sibling is slightly older than him."[3]

Einstein also demonstrated that measurements of spacetime are relative to the motion of an observer. Einstein's theory of special relativity shows that a stationary observer will find that the length of a fast-moving object is less than if the object was at rest. Also the passage of time on the fast-moving object is actually slower than if the object was at rest. Conversely for an observer inside the fast-moving object everything inside is its normal length and time passes normally. However, for this observer lengths of objects in the outside world are shortened, and time in the outside world is running slow. In other words, measurements of space and time taken by an observer will be different for a stationary observer and a moving observer.

Einstein demonstrated that measurements of time and space are relative to the motion of an observer. There is a relativity in our experience of the physical world – except when it comes to the measurement of the speed of light. In Einstein s discoveries the speed of light itself remains constant. The measured speed of light in a vacuum is the same whether or not the source of the light and the measuring device are moving relative to one another.

The speed of light is the defining limit in spacetime. "Another consequence of Special Relativity is that *nothing* can travel faster than the speed of light. Any object with mass moving near the speed of light would experience an increase in its mass. That mass would approach infinity as it reached light speed and would, therefore, require an infinite amount of energy to accelerate it to light speed. The fastest possible speed any form of information or force (including gravity) can operate is at the speed of light."[4] How extraordinary it must have been to discover that light has a speed and that so much of our physical experience (including of gravity) is defined by it.

However, as we shall see, the advent of quantum theory would unveil a much more relative, and altogether stranger world. Even as Einstein's predictions were being proved to be true, new theories were suggesting that physical objects could behave in a manner previously considered scientifically impossible and could be connected with each other in a manner that defied the speed of light rule. Let's enter the strange world of quantum mechanics where things are not what they seem.

2. Quantum Mechanics and Quantum Entanglement

In the early 20th century physicists made new discoveries that further undermined the certainties of classical physics. The laws discovered by Newton and Einstein are applicable to large objects in space as well as to fields spread out in space but don't stand up in the world of the very small – the world of photons and electrons. At this very small scale, physicists discovered, it was much harder to make definitive measurements and predictions of how something would behave. Physicists like Heisenberg and Bohr concluded that physical systems at the micro level, such as electrons and photons, exist as sets of probabilities, only taking on definite properties in the act of measurement.

The question of the existence of an objective reality, defined by its own laws and behaving in a predictable fashion whether it was being measured or not, probably never arose for Newton. In the view of classical physics the world existed like a machine, defined by laws of motion and gravitation. It was thought that this world, set in motion originally by the Creator, was like a vast machine in which an observer had no agency and which was, once the laws governing it were understood, entirely predictable in its functioning.

With the advent of quantum theory the certainties of Newton's world and the formulations of Einstein were called into question. Although their theories were valid, and held up experimentally in most situations, it was found that they didn't hold up in *all* situations. Heisenberg and others showed that at the micro level you couldn't separate the observed from the observer in a clear-cut way. It was beginning to seem that the "entire experimental setup", including all observers and experimental equipment, couldn't be separated from observed outcomes of experiments. Observed outcomes depended on experimental conditions, devices and observations. In time, some quantum theorists would go even further, proposing that measured outcomes are the result, not just of the experimental set up, measuring devices and so on, but, even more radically, of the presence of an observing human consciousness.

Welcome to the strange and unpredictable world of quantum mechanics. Here's some of what the early quantum pioneers found when they probed into the sub-atomic structure of matter.

Quantum objects such as electrons and photons can behave like waves or particles. Indeed they can be both. Particles in experimental situations such as the double slit experiment (one of the most famous experiments in physics) are seen to have wave-like qualities.[5] Yet when these apparent waves are observed in a different way they again behave like particles. The act of observing or measuring a quantum system has an effect on the system, on what is observed. This constitutes the measurement problem of quantum mechanics. But the argument that changes in the observed properties of quantum objects are due only to the disturbing effects of experimental equipment has been disproved many times. Such changes are apparently more to do with the fact of observation than with disturbances caused by equipment.

Einstein had already made the bold proposition that light could be a particle. Actually Newton had proposed the same thing, but subsequently, with the discovery of electromagnetic fields, light had been thought of as a wave. Now here was Einstein proposing that light could come in packets, quantum objects soon to be named photons. Once this had been established it wasn't long before matter itself, which was currently considered at the scale of the very tiny to consist of quantum objects such as electrons, would be shown, like light, to have both particle and wave properties.

At the scale of quantum objects, things are not fixed. Heisenberg's *uncertainty principle* demonstrates that you cannot predict the position and momentum of a quantum object at the same time. The more you know about one property the less you know about the other.

Quantum objects seem to exist as "probability waves" until measured. It's not possible to predict, but only to give a probability of finding an actual particle in a certain place at a certain time. In a sense, the particle is in all the places that it could have been potentially seen until it is measured. Quantum objects are said to be in a superposition state until measured or observed. At this point things take on a definite value. A probability becomes an actual thing. This is the so-called collapse of the wave function.[6] In quantum theory the wave function doesn't exist in any well-defined state until someone makes an observation and collapses the wave function. Until then you have the superposition of all possible states.

Things get even more uncertain. There is much debate as to what constitutes an observer. Some say that it's the measuring device – itself a quantum object consisting of atoms, etc. Others maintain that it's consciousness itself – the act of conscious witnessing – that collapses the wave function, that causes something in a superpositional state to take on specific attributes. A further question would then be, what constitutes consciousness? Could it be human, or a cat, or an amoeba, or an inanimate object devised and used by human researchers such as a measuring device?[7]

Then there's the question of the actual objective existence of a probability wave. Things exist as a probability wave until measured and particles with definite properties appear. "There are two prominent interpretations of the wave function dating back to its origins in the 1920s. In one view, the wave function corresponds to an element of reality that objectively exists whether or not an observer is measuring it. In an alternative view, the wave function does not represent reality but instead represents an observer's subjective state of knowledge about some underlying reality. In 1927, Niels Bohr and others advocated this alternative view in the Copenhagen interpretation, in which the wave function is merely a mathematical probability that immediately assumes only one value when an observer measures the system, resulting in the wave function collapsing. Still others disagree with both views."[8] In a sense then, the Copenhagen interpretation suggests that human subjectivity plays a part in observed states of matter in experimental situations.

No wonder the most famous physicist of recent times, Richard Feynman, reportedly stated "I think I can safely say that nobody understands quantum mechanics."

Quantum entanglement

Quantum experiments had demonstrated that quantum objects such as electrons or photons don't exist as well-defined objects with specific attributes of momentum, position, spin and so on, until they are measured. Evidence suggests that, at the quantum level, reality consists of probability waves. In other words, things exist in a superpositional state until they are looked at, measured, witnessed. Then they take on specific properties in an event physicists dub the "collapse of the wavefunction".

So much for quantum objects and for the discoveries that in the early 20th century rocked the foundations of our ideas about, and perceptions of, physical reality.

But things were about to get stranger still. It would be shown that such quantum objects not only took on attributes only when measured or seen, but somehow communicated this event to other quantum objects in a manner that defied all current understanding of how the physical universe worked

One theory that arose from quantum mechanics, a theory that would eventually be confirmed by experimental data, suggested that once two particles had been combined in a single system – for example a pair of photons that had been emitted from an atom – those two particles would remain entangled no matter how far apart they were removed. To say that two particles are entangled means that if you separate the two particles, no matter by what distance and perform a measurement on one of them, the other one will also respond to the measurement simultaneously. (It has since been shown that entanglement can also occur between larger entangled systems such as electrons, atoms and even small molecules).

It is as if the measured behaviour of one particle had been immediately (simultaneously) communicated to the other particle in the absence of any causal mechanism or signal that would make this possible. If the two particles responded simultaneously, that is without any measurable time delay, to a measurement performed on only one of the particles, it meant that any such communication between them could not be due to electromagnetic signalling because, as we have noted, Einstein had shown that such communication couldn't travel faster than the speed of light. And yet here was something – a simultaneous action at a distance connecting two particles – that defied that law. Einstein believed that what was being proposed was impossible. He famously remarked that these connections couldn't be due to "spooky action at a distance". They must instead be due, he proposed, to as yet undiscovered "hidden variables" which would predetermine the behaviour of such entangled particles. Since these variables – unknown predetermining factors in the behaviour of particles – were as yet undiscovered, quantum theory must be, he maintained, incomplete.

Hidden variables

Einstein was especially troubled by one prediction of quantum theory. As we've seen, the Copenhagen interpretation of quantum mechanics (advanced by Niels Bohr and Werner Heisenberg) states that physical reality, at the quantum level, cannot be said to maintain an objective existence independent of the presence of a measuring device or observer. Matter is in a superpositional state (where all possibilities exist) until, under the act of observation, particles take on specific properties of position, momentum or spin.

Albert Einstein, along with two colleagues, Boris Podolsky and Nathan Rosen, set to thinking about this and realised that quantum theory must therefore predict some very strange outcomes. This thought experiment is known as the EPR paradox (after the three physicists).

Let's look at the first part of their argument. This involves a pair of entangled particles. The term entangled had not yet been coined. But in this imagined experiment, two particles that have been part of a single system –

for example two photons that have been emitted from an atom – are separated to some distance from each other. And it's important to note here that in theory this distance can be close, like the next room, or vast, as on the other side of the galaxy. The actual distance is immaterial.

Now, according to known laws of physics, these two particles must always maintain opposite values. This means that if you measure a value of particle A, you will automatically know the value of particle B because it has to be opposite.

Let's take spin as an example. I should say that particles are not spinning like little planets. But particles do have magnetic properties, creating magnetic fields. At one time it was believed that particles must therefore be spinning. This has since been shown to be impossible. But the term has stuck, and particles are said to have spin up or spin down. In fact particles are now thought of as more like a point in space, rather than an object.

But laws of conservation say that overall values of the universe, such as charge or spin, will stay constant. For example, because the charge of the universe is conserved (stays constant), every particle must have an antiparticle, thus conserving charge. (Put simply, opposites must always balance each other out). This means, returning to our two particles, that measuring the first as having spin up, automatically means the second will have spin down.

So far so good. But there's a problem. Remember that according to quantum theory particles are in a state of superposition, only taking on definite properties in the act of measurement. Here's the paradox. Particle A is undecided until measured. It has all possibilities. So it has both spin up *and* spin down. *But,* at the same time, we know that particle B will, the moment particle A is measured, instantly take the opposite value to that of particle A.

The EPR thought experiment concluded that this led to an impossible result. Einstein and his colleagues pointed out that quantum theory leads to the conclusion that the act of measurement on particle A, at which point it takes on its values, must be instantaneously communicated to particle B, defying Einstein's theory of relativity which states that nothing travels faster than the speed of light. What makes this conclusion inevitable?

The wavefunction of both particles must collapse simultaneously in order that the opposite values of the two particles be maintained. What could happen if this wasn't the case? If there was a time delay, as Einstein's light speed law stipulates, in the communication between particle A and particle B, then in theory in this time delay period another measurement could be performed on particle B which gets a different result. The later measurement on particle B would give a 50/50 chance of being spin up or spin down. In other words, if particle A was spin up, particle B could also collapse to spin up when a later measurement is performed on it, meaning the overall constant of the universe would no longer be maintained.

So communication must be instantaneous. But such communication is impossible. This is why Einstein claimed that quantum theory must be incomplete. Incomplete because it can't explain all the facts.

Let's return to hidden variables. What Einstein is proposing here is that particle A does not, and cannot, communicate its properties to particle B in some spookily instantaneous manner. At the same time this communication would have to be instantaneous in order to ensure that the opposite values of the two particles were preserved. Satisfying both requirements simultaneously – nothing travels faster than light, and opposite values must be maintained – is impossible. What he proposes instead is that hidden variables must be at work. The two particles must already have specific values of position, momentum or spin, before being measured and independently of observation. They must have certain objectively existing values according to underlying predetermining factors existing at the time they were part of one system. These values must objectively and independently be there, whether we observe them or not. Outcomes are already decided in advance. However, we cannot know all the factors that went to produce the outcome. We cannot know all the variables at work, which nevertheless produce the observed outcome. Thus particles are being influenced in ways that are both variable and hidden (from the observer's point of view).

In Einstein's view there is nothing spooky about the second particle instantaneously showing opposite spin, since the values of the particles already exist. If the spin of particle A was already up, independent of observation, then the spin of particle B must be down, as it will always be opposite. He thought of it something like this. Imagine two boxes. Inside one there is a red marble, inside the other a green one. The values of the marbles (red, green) are already there whether we see them or not. So when you open one box and find the red marble, you immediately know that the other marble in the other box is green. Nothing spooky. Just discovering what was already there. But this goes right to the heart of the argument between Einstein and the quantum theorists. Quantum theory, later to be backed by evidence, stated that values of red or green don't exist until the box is opened. Until then both marbles are both red and green. Einstein, perhaps the last of the great classicists, was having none of it.

Bell's Theorem

This chapter is the most technical and I'm now going to introduce physicist John Bell's proof that particles can indeed be in instantaneous correlation with each other. If you don't want more detail you can skip this and go straight to chapter 3.

Things had reached stalemate. Quantum theory maintained that particles such as electrons existed in a superpositional state until measured. Only at the moment of measurement or observation, with the collapse of the wavefunction, do particles take on specific values, such as those of position, momentum or spin.

Einstein, on the other hand, had proposed that particles must already have their properties, prior to measurement and independent of observation. According to Einstein things exist intrinsically in a classical state. Things are as they are, whether we witness them or not. Whether we know them or not.

Who was right? In 1935 there was no equipment and no experiment which could put an end to this argument by showing which side was correct. Things were left in this unsatisfactory state for nearly thirty years, until a Scottish physicist working at the world-famous CERN laboratory took up the challenge.

John Bell became fascinated by the unsolved problem left by Einstein and the quantum theorists. He devised the following thought experiment with the intention of settling the matter. Suppose you had a source of quantum particles that, once emitted, set off in opposite directions. These two particles then encounter separate measuring devices which can measure the spin of each particle along 3 separate axes: one, two and three. Each measuring device can choose at random along which axis of the particle it will perform its measurement. And there's really no way for one measuring device to know what the other is doing. As well as that, the choice of which axis to measure is made *after* the particle has been sent on its journey. So the particle couldn't know in advance what measurement will be selected.

Now this is where the statistics come in. Let's call the measuring devices Alice's measuring device and Bob's measuring device. If both particles happen to be measured along the same axis (both measuring devices select axis one, for example), the spins will always be opposite (spin up and spin down). If Alice has chosen axis one, then Bob can randomly choose axis one, two or three. So opposite spin should occur one third of the time (i.e. when Bob happens to choose axis one) when the experiment is repeated many times with Alice measuring axis one.

But if Bob happens to measure along axis two or three, statistically he will get the same spin as Alice *more often than not*. More often than not, statistically, *where no communication is happening between the particles* both Alice and Bob will get the same result – both spin up or both spin down. If Alice and Bob are on the same axis they will always get opposite spin. But if

Alice remains on axis one, and Bob randomly chooses two or three, more often than not both will get the same spin. If you put all this together, statistically the overall result is 50/50. Alice and Bob *should* get the same result 50% of the time – both spin up or both spin down – and the opposite result 50% of the time – one spin up and one spin down.

If both particles are measured along the same axis – axis one for example – laws of conservation mean you will get opposite spin 100% of the time.

But if you do *all possible combinations* of Alice's three directions and Bob's three directions, statistically you will find, when the experiment is repeated many times, results are opposite (spin up and spin down) 5 out of 9 times.

So here's the point. If each particle is already set in advance (while still part of its original system), if it already knows what spin it has before measurement, then when both particles are measured along the same axis they will have opposite spins 100% of the the time. And when you take all combinations of Alice and Bob randomly selecting which axis they will measure (each one randomly selecting axis 1, 2 or 3), and repeat the experiment many times, you should see that you get opposite spins (up and down) 5 out of 9 times.

When you put all this together (*measurements on the same axis and all possible combinations of measurements on the three axes*) you should get opposite spin *more than five out of nine times*. Statistically this is what should happen if the particles are not in 'spooky communication'.

But this isn't what the thought experiment comes up with, and isn't what happened in actual experiments. In experiments you only get opposite results 50% of the the time. So Bell had demonstrated that the particles couldn't have been set in advance independent of observation. But he hadn't started with that assumption.

He started his thought experiment with the assumption that hidden variables could explain the facts of quantum entanglement. He started with Einstein's view that particles had already taken on properties prior to and independent of observations, even though those properties are unknown to the observer and are thus designated "hidden variables". But that's not where he ended up. He showed through his thought experiment that this view couldn't explain the facts. Only a model of reality in which instantaneous connection between points removed from each other in space could explain the facts. And yes, this conclusion was eventually supported by experimental evidence. This evidence confirmed the view that any model of reality now had to allow for instantaneous (or at least faster than light) connections.

In the 1960s this was still all theory. It was thought experiment pitted against thought experiment in the absence of equipment sensitive and fast enough to perform such experiments on entangled particles. But this would change and scientists would build the equipment to put Bell's hypothesis to the test. Starting with John Clauser in the 1970s and Alain Aspect in the 1980s, laboratory experiments have shown with increasing certainty that John Bell was right. The correlation of entangled particles in which a measurement on particle A immediately affects both particle A and particle B cannot be explained by laws of cause and effect and cannot be explained by the hypothesis of hidden variables, in which particles had already taken on values before they were measured.

Before we finish this section there's one more theory that should be mentioned. David Bohm's 'pilot wave' theory. David Bohm is a physicist whose ideas I will draw on extensively later in the book. But just now let's look at a theory he proposed early in his career.

Bohm had espoused the Copenhagen interpretation of quantum data, as proposed by Heisenberg and Bohr. An interpretation that maintains that matter at the micro level is in a superpositional state, only taking on specific properties in the act of measurement – the collapse of the wavefunction. However, in discussion with Einstein he was convinced otherwise. So he proposed a theory that could be consistent with observed facts as well as with a theory of hidden variables. He tried to create a model of reality in which particles would have objective values independent of observers or experimental devices. He took his cue from ideas proposed, but not fully developed, in the 1920s by physicist Louis de Broglie, who had been one of the first to propose that matter, like light, could be wave as well as particle.

The De Broglie-Bohm pilot wave theory, sometimes known as Bohmian mechanics, proposes real waves (there is debate as to whether the wavefunction is a real wave or a kind of mathematical abstraction) that push around real particles. These particles have definite properties such as location, velocity or spin – objective properties existing independently of observation. Particles are guided by a real wave. They aren't in a superpositional state until measured, but have objective values independent of observation. Like Einstein he wanted to show that there's an objective world independent of observation. As the well-known aphorism goes, the tree falling in the forest still makes a sound, even if there's no one there to hear it.

Pilot wave theory was able to meet some of the important requirements of quantum mechanics. For example particles, according to this theory, would still produce a wave pattern in the double-slit experiment. But pilot wave theory could also support Einstein's idea of hidden variables. In the pilot wave version of events this means that although quantum objects have properties independent of observation, we still cannot know what they are because of tiny and unknown variables in measurement procedures, or because any measurement causes a disturbance (the pilot wave responds to anything and everything). So apparent randomness arises in connection with measuring procedures, even though a particle has objective values guided by the pilot wave. But there's a big problem.

According to physicist Nick Herbert: "In Bohm's model the electron is a particle, having at all times a definite position and momentum. In addition, each electron is connected to a new field – the so-called 'pilot wave' – which guides its movement according to a new law of motion. Both wave and particle are real – no fictitious proxy waves here – but the pilot wave is invisible, observable only indirectly via its effects on its electron."[9]

He continues: "The pilot wave, acting as a sort of probe of the environment, changes its shape instantly whenever a change occurs anywhere in the world. In turn, pilot wave communicates news of this to electron, which alters its position and momentum. When you make one kind of measurement, the pilot wave has one form; when you make another kind of measurement, this wave takes another form. For different kinds of measurement the electron takes on different attributes, because its pilot wave is different."

Now here comes the punchline: "However, Bohm's model is plagued with a peculiar affliction. In order for it to work, whenever something changes anywhere the pilot wave has to inform the electron instantly of this change, which necessitates faster-than-light signalling."[10]

So "Bohm's pilot wave puts the electron in instant contact with every other particle in the universe" and "an entity that can instantly change its properties in response to a tiny change made half a universe away is no ordinary object."[11]

So pilot wave theory agrees with many of the predictions of quantum mechanics but manages to preserve real objects and waves independent of the activity of observers. But this wave connects everything anywhere, or even everywhere, instantaneously. So we're back to the same problem encountered with quantum entanglement. Instantaneous connection between distant objects that defies the laws of physics enshrined in Einstein's theories of relativity.

However, we could see in Bohm's theory an early attempt to formulate a model of a universal field, which accounts for observed facts, and in which all apparently separate objects have the possibility to be in instantaneous connection with each other. A model in which time and space don't exist in the way we normally experience them. A model that describes a non-physical field that can't be known directly, is instantaneously responsive to any movement anywhere in the universe, and which instantly communicates that movement everywhere as well as to any particular part.

Locality and Non-Locality

Bell's theorem, along with the experimental evidence that followed, could suggest that the basic order underlying reality is not one of separate objects obeying laws that guide their behaviour regardless of and separate from any observer. His theory, along with subsequent experiments, suggests that the reality underlying the world we experience through our senses could be more 'non-local' than 'local'. In physics, when reality is described as local it means that events separated from each other in space and time have a local effect on each other. Something in one region of time and space has an effect on something else in another region of time and space. This could be when physical objects interact with one another, for example when two snooker balls collide, or when one molecule has a chemical effect on another, or when a sensory stimulus leads to nerve activity. In this localised reality things can also act upon each other via fields through which waves are propagated, as when light waves from a source are propagated through an electromagnetic field and stimulate the eye's retina. However, in this local description of physical reality no influence or signal can travel faster than the speed of light. Time is always involved and thus time and space are indissolubly wedded.

In the non-local description of reality, things are not so definably separate in space and time. Quantum theory had uncovered the mysterious fact that objects apparently completely separate in spacetime can maintain a non-local connection with each other. Remember, local influences cannot pass between location A and location B faster than the speed of light. Whereas in non-locality, events separate in space can appear to be connected instantaneously, as for example in the simultaneous behaviour of two entangled photons.

The notion of locality suggests a world in which measurable influences, effects or signals between locations separated in space and time form the fundamental physical reality. In this reality objects and events are separate in space and time, and influence each other via signals (such as electromagnetic or gravitational waves) travelling no faster than the speed of light. On the other hand, the notion of non-locality suggests an underlying reality that isn't primarily one of separate bits. Apparently separate things could be connected in a kind of unity. The facts of instantaneous quantum correlations could point to something more fundamental than the reality of apparently separate objects. In fact, as we shall see, this more fundamental reality may be thought of as whole and undivided, appearing as localised – that is to say as consisting of objects separate one from another in space and time – only under certain conditions.

We shall see that according to theorists like David Bohm there is an underlying reality, as it were behind the world of separate things, that isn't localised at all. Rather it is an unbroken whole, undefined by space and time, and yet containing the potential of any possible separate thing. Seemingly separate objects and events with specific properties appear out of, and merge back into, an underlying unity.

In the pre-quantum scientific view of reality, separate things follow specific laws and have local effects on each other. But Bell showed that the basic reality could be non-local. Quantum theory, supported by Bell's theorem, showed a reality where distant objects can be simultaneously connected without any possibility or need for a signal passing between such objects (occupying different regions of space).[12] This suggests the possibility of a unified, unbroken underlying reality – a reality that is essentially whole and not made of separate bits.

At the same time as developments in the world of quantum physics, the psychologist C. G. Jung was making, from a different perspective, his own observations and drawing his own conclusions about spacetime, and about locality and non-locality. He was formulating his theory of synchronicity.

3. Synchronicity

We know from published archive material that between 1932 and 1958 Jung was in correspondence with the respected physicist Wolfgang Pauli (a key physicist in the early days of quantum theory), and so was aware of developments in the field of quantum physics. In fact, Jung and Pauli collaborated extensively to try to understand a possible common ground for physics and depth psychology. This joint research followed Pauli's request to Jung for psychological help. Pauli in fact entered extensive analysis, sometimes with Jung and sometimes with other Jungian analysts recommended by Jung. Whatever the influence the two men may have had on one another, during the first half of the 20ᵗʰ century, working in his own field, Jung was attempting to show that events separated in space and time could be meaningfully connected even in the absence of causal links. His work on synchronicity, *Synchronicity: an acausal connecting principle,* was first published in 1960.[13] Here I'll just outline his findings and conclusions.

His own experience, as well as data from his clinical practice, suggested that events can be connected in a significant and demonstrable manner in the absence of obvious causal links. In support of his hypothesis Jung gives consideration to recorded examples of telepathy and precognition. He suggests that the evidence for telepathy, precognition and reports of other similar inexplicable" phenomena cannot be ignored. Researchers such as Rupert Sheldrake have, through their own experiments, done much to substantiate these views. Jung also cites the well-documented experiments conducted by J.B. Rhine in the 1930s in which subjects, under controlled conditions, had to guess which cards were being turned up from specially designed packs by experimenters. Results in these tests were significantly above statistical expectation. If the tests did indeed show some kind of link between card, experimenter and test subject, how could this link be facilitated in the absence of any known causal link? (It should be pointed out that scientists often dismiss the results of such tests, citing flaws in the test protocols or maintaining that results can be put down to chance or statistical averages.)

Jung also points out that if someone has precognition of events *yet* to occur, or a test subject is able to guess (with results well above statistical average) the image on a card that has *yet* to be turned up (i.e. the subject guesses the design on the card before the card is turned up), then it appears that we're dealing with connected events separate not only in space, but in time as well – i.e. the future affecting the present. (The Rhine experiments were designed mainly to test whether subjects would be able to guess the design on a card which *had* been turned up – but some were designed to see if the subject could detect the design on a card *before* it was turned up.)

Jung then goes on to tell the now famous story of his patient who dreamt of a scarab beetle, the Egyptian dung beetle. He had been despairing of the possibility of making headway with this particular patient whose rather fixed attitudes seemed to be preventing progress.

One day she came with a dream of a golden scarab beetle that had occurred the night before. As she related this already significant dream, Jung heard a tapping at the window behind him. He got up and saw to his surprise an insect knocking against the glass in an attempt to get into the darker room (interestingly the insect was going from a lighter environment to a darker – the opposite of what you'd expect). He opened the window and, as it flew in, caught it in his hand and saw that it was a rose chafer (*Cetonia aurata*), a greenish gold beetle of the Scarabaeidae family – the representative commonly found in Northern Europe of the same family to which the Egyptian scarab beetle belongs. He showed it to the patient exclaiming "here is your scarab beetle!" He reports that somehow this event produced a shift in the patient which allowed the therapy to proceed successfully.[14]

In his essay on synchronicity, Jung is careful to emphasise several key points. To say that synchronicity is at work we have to rule out any causal link between two events. In the story of the dream, the dream beetle didn't *cause* the beetle to appear at the window the next day. (Of course, various causal explanations could be found for the beetle's behaviour. However, Jung suggests that acausal connections can be associated with or "carried by" causal connections, reminding us that both explanations could be true.[15]) We also need to distinguish between something being synchronistic, meaning a true example of synchronicity, and things being synchronous, meaning that two or more events are merely chance coincidences.

Jung has proposed that events that are connected with each other through synchronicity, rather than through a cause and effect or chance connection, are in some way "meaningfully connected". What are we to make of this? Clearly if something is meaningful, it has to be meaningful or significant to somebody. So synchronistic events must include a 'somebody', a subject. But this subject isn't merely a neutral bystander. Their subjectivity is somehow involved in the events. In his essay Jung suggests that for such meaningfully connected events to 'show up' in a spacetime world often characterised by causal links and chance coincidences, the unconscious of the subject needs to be constellated.

In Jung's terms this means an archetype is activated or "constellated". According to Jung an archetype is a kind of primary pattern that underlies events and situations, as well as our experience of things. Things fall into patterns. You can't know an archetype directly, only through its effects. Let me offer an image to help think about this: a vortex of water in a river. What do you see? You see the water. But the water is moving in a pattern. But you can only know the pattern as it shows up in the movement of the water. The motion of forces in the flow of the water produces the dynamic spiral pattern that the water takes. We can then extrapolate the idea of the spiral form from the situation of the water. We might then notice other natural phenomena that take a spiral form – clouds, plants, snail shells, galaxies for example. So in this simple example, we might think of the spiral form as an archetype, which we only see when it shows itself through a particular medium – river, cloud, plant, shell, galaxy. The spiral itself, removed from its medium of expression, is a kind of ideal form that takes on different modes of expression in nature. Such a spiral itself can be shown to have certain geometric or mathematical proportions.

Wherever we look in nature we see underlying patterns – in crystals, in plants, in animals, and in the nebulae far out in the cosmos. Also the study of human beings, human history and human culture reveals common underlying patterns at work. That's why, for example, comparative ethnologists such as Jung and Joseph Campbell were able to discern similar themes and motifs in the great mythic stories appearing in different cultures and different historical periods. They arise from a common source – from fundamental patterns underlying individual and cultural perception and activity.

As we'll soon see, it's possible that such patterns transcend space and time. That is to say they are not confined or defined by spacetime laws. Archetypal patterns may be more non-local in their effects, than local. If that's the case then the apparent division between 'inner' and 'outer' may not hold up either. In synchronistic events, if such patterns are in some way activated, then they may manifest inwardly and outwardly simultaneously. Thus a connection could exist between the inner state or condition of an individual and outer events: a connection for which no causal explanation can be found.

Jung writes: "The meaningful coincidence or equivalence of a psychic and a physical state that have no causal relationship to one another means, in general terms, that it is a modality without a cause, an 'acausal orderedness'. The question now arises whether our definition of synchronicity with reference to the equivalence of psychic and physical processes is capable of expansion. This requirement seems to force itself on us when we consider the above, wider conception of synchronicity as an 'acausal orderedness'."[16]

The idea of an "acausal orderedness" – an order not limited by the laws of cause and effect and therefore unlimited by spacetime – is something we'll be returning to more, even if the terminology used is slightly different.

An archetype can be thought of as a fundamental pattern showing up both in our subjective world of perceptions, dreams, thoughts and sensations, as well as in the external world of actual events. "For the archetype is the introspectively recognizable form of *a priori* psychic orderedness. If an external synchronistic process now associates itself with it, it falls into the same basic pattern – in other words, it too is 'ordered'."[17]

But Jung maintains that this activation of an archetypal pattern needs certain conditions. This means that the person who experiences or is present to these events is more "activated" in some way. Maybe there's a more or less pressing need for change, for a new way of being. One might say something is primed, is ready. This readiness, this expectation, in as much as it's more or less unconscious, can somehow constellate synchronistic events – events that are meaningfully and significantly connected, but have no demonstrable causal link. After all, the dream beetle didn't cause the real beetle to appear. But the dream did perhaps occur in a charged atmosphere of frustration, even if unconscious. In a synchronistic occurrence the interior psychic state of a person is entwined or, borrowing from the language of quantum mechanics, entangled or correlated with objective reality. And for this to happen, there has to be, even if more or less unconscious, a condition of need or expectation.

Synchronistic events are meaningful in the sense that they can alert us to something. They can wake something up in us. They might somehow remind us that our limited view of reality is not all there is. If, for whatever reason, there is a relaxation of the conscious hold, we encounter a liminal world, in which the structure of spacetime isn't so fixed. Unforeseen solutions to problems might apparently come from nowhere. Or we might have intimations of events before they happen. Our perceptions become less limited by the structure of spacetime. Or rather the structure of our limited perceptions dissolves or breaks down. We enter liminal spacetime.

In such conditions it's as if something that 'knows' more than we do, in our limited view of reality, breaks through our constructed, causal world. We become connected to a larger reality, where division in space and between past and future is more permeable. These are the more fluid conditions conducive to a perception of meaningfully and acausally connected events. (For more on Jung's use of the term *meaning*, see final chapter).

I should add here that Sheldrake and other contemporary researchers don't consider the experience of such acausally connected phenomena as paranormal. Rather they relate to natural faculties which allow connections with a larger reality. These faculties are part of nature and part of the survival capacity of living organisms. It's easy to see how advanced knowing, for example, would enhance the survival ability of animals or humans.

Returning to entanglement, I'm not of course suggesting that a person is entangled, in the literal meaning of entanglement, with external events. In the observations of quantum mechanics the largest objects shown to be entangled with each other are small molecules such as those of Buckminsterfullerene – small carbon molecules. But we are considering phenomena in which there appears to be a meaningful connection between inner and outer events, despite the absence of any known electromagnetic signals that could link such events. For example, if someone has precognition of an event yet to happen, then the two events (the precognition and the actual event) are synchronistically linked, rather than being linked through any known causal signal.

The card-guessing experiments cited above also show an acausal link between inner and outer events – in this case between the perceptions of the subject of the experiment (inner) and the designs on the cards (outer). This link is acausal in that there's no scientific (in the narrow sense of the term) explanation for any kind of transmission. But if the card-guessing experiments do demonstrate acausal links – results that are statistically more significant than chance – then what about the element of "meaningfulness" that Jung suggests should be present if synchronicity is to occur? Surely such a random and rather meaningless experimental situation such as that found in the Rhine experiments couldn't be said to be meaningful? Jung's comment is surprising. He suggests that the acausal link between these things (subject, experimenter and card) found in the Rhine experiments could indeed be said to be meaningful. He asks us to consider the fact that these experimenters were engaged in a highly unusual experiment, the results of which, if confirmed, could rock the very foundations of the, then current, scientific understanding of the world. This could be said to be meaningful. Is it possible that the unconscious of the test subjects was indeed aroused in the charged-with-significance atmosphere of the experiments? Actually Jung supports this contention, and notes the observation that when test subjects in the Rhine experiments lost interest or became bored their success rate was observed to diminish. Only when enthusiasm was reactivated did their results improve again.

We can begin to see then that such demonstrations of acausal or non-local connections found in synchronicity and similar phenomena are not merely objective occurrences. They demonstrate the interpenetration of subjective and objective realities. To borrow from Buddhist terminology, inner and outer co-arise. The subjective state can't be avoided or overlooked.

From the perspective of contemporary science, all such phenomena discussed here are illusory. They can't be happening. This is because large parts of scientific orthodoxy cannot allow the possibility of the involvement of subjective states. Science needs to separate the objective from the subjective in order to build a knowledge base as free as possible from changing or arbitrary subjective states of human experimenters. (I'll return to this important point more fully in the final chapter.) But the study of events apparently acausally linked suggests that this hard line between inner and outer is not as absolute or real as scientists might like to believe.

The view suggested here also throws light on the fact that experimental endeavours such as the Rhine experiments are hard to replicate. When replication fails, perhaps due to a changed or unfavourable psychic or physical environment, critics merely say "I told you so" and dismiss the whole experimental endeavour as erroneous or fraudulent.

The point I'm emphasising here is that synchronistic events (events that are meaningfully, but acausally, connected) don't just occur in neutral conditions. They occur in conditions of need, expectation, excitement, longing and so on. The element of passion and need has to be present. The full force of the subjectivity of an involved subject is present. This means that fundamental pre-rational drives and needs are indeed involved, further confirming to many scientists the irrationality of such a view of reality. The current scientific paradigm cannot admit such an interplay of inner and outer realities. So the scientific mind concludes that all such events are illusory; that all statistics that show such events could occur are the product of fraud or error. That researchers of such things are themselves embedded in magical thinking.

What about quantum correlations? Could we even approach such a hard scientific fact from the perspective we're taking here? The fact remains that particles can be correlated in the absence of any known cause-and-effect mechanism. Could such correlations have first occurred in an unusually constellated psychic environment where powerful unconscious forces were at work? (And, as we'll see in the next chapter, once such correlation has occurred a kind of 'habit' would be established that would allow them to go on occurring independent of a changing psychic environment. Their occurrence would, so to speak, become an independent fact.) Could it be said then that such correlations are also examples of meaningful connection? What about the early days of quantum mechanics and the findings that began to emerge in the first quarter of the 20th century? Was there then an environment, in the research centres of Europe and America, of high unconscious charge? After all, the early quantum experiments were making world-shaking discoveries, profoundly challenging the accepted view of reality, in a Europe already being shaken to its very foundations by unprecedented change, turmoil and destruction. These scientists were not on neutral ground! A more highly charged psychic, and even spiritual, environment is hard to imagine.

If anyone doubts the capacity of psychic states of hope, expectation and belief to play a significant role in objective events, then they need only turn to the large body of placebo evidence. Although placebo studies are beyond the scope of this book, I make passing reference to them here.[18]

It has been shown that effects on an individual's health, sometimes dramatic, can be significantly enhanced or altered by such factors as the colour of a placebo pill (or indeed the colour of real medication), or whether a placebo is given as a pill or as an injection. Cultural precedents and faith in the ability of the medical practitioner are also among many other factors that allow the administration of inert medications to produce positive changes in the physical and mental health of individuals.

Objective changes (in this case in a person's physical health) occur in conditions of subjective readiness (inner psychological states characterised by hope, expectation and so on). Placebo studies don't necessarily demonstrate the activity of events that are synchronistic – that is to say acausally and meaningfully connected. Placebo effects are usually thought to be due to such factors as cues unconsciously picked up by subjects in drug trials for example. The colour of a medication or the manner of an authority figure in the trial, such as a doctor, can trigger responses in a trial subject that can show up as a biophysical as well as a psychological effect. But at the very least such effects demonstrate the interconnection between inner (psychological) and outer (changes in physical health) events.

However it may also be the case that placebo activity can have a synchronistic element to it. This synchronistic element would allow participants in drug trials to be non-locally influenced by each other and by health professionals overseeing the trials. Such effects could then take place at a distance and would be independent of the more obvious placebo effects arising through the physical proximity of a trial subject to a drug or authority figure. If such non-local effects are present in drug trials it would raise many further questions in our understanding of the placebo effect. And it would indicate again that causal explanations, such as the power of suggestion being responsible for a placebo effect in a drug trial, could exist alongside an acausal explanation of placebo effects, namely non-local connections between trial participants.

Jung himself was aware of the weight of objections against all that was being proposed, despite the anecdotal evidence passed down through history – for clairvoyance, precognition and so on. And despite the extraordinary findings of the early pioneers of quantum mechanics, and despite the record of his own research. "Meaningful coincidences are thinkable as pure chance. But the more they multiply and the greater and more exact the correspondence is, the more their probability sinks and their unthinkability increases, until they can no longer be regarded as pure chance but, for lack of a causal explanation, have to be thought of as meaningful arrangements. As I have already said, however, their 'inexplicability' is not due to the fact that the cause is unknown, but to the fact that a cause is not even thinkable in intellectual terms. This is necessarily the case when space and time lose their meaning or have become relative, for under those circumstances a causality which presupposes space and time for its continuance can no longer be said to exist and becomes altogether unthinkable."[19]

When space and time lose their meaning or have become relative. Let's continue to explore these ideas in the next chapter, where I consider more fully the role of similarity.

4. Similarity

The dictionary defines 'similar' as "having a resemblance in appearance, character, or quality, without being identical". We can think of examples of similarity. An orange is similar to a grapefruit. An orange is even more similar to another orange, though the two are not identical. Brothers may be more or less similar to each other. An English ten-pound note is similar to a US ten-dollar bill – similar but not identical. A ten-dollar bill is not similar to an orange. A portrait is similar to the person depicted, but not identical.

In our perception similarity creates a kind of connection between things. It plays a role in memory, in recall and in recognition. So similarity makes the relationship between things accessible to us.

Here's another pointer for similarity. We can quite easily say what's similar to an orange, but can we say what's opposite to an orange? Try it. You might be able to say what's opposite to one quality of an orange – its roundness, its colour, its smell and so on. But can you say what's opposite to the whole orange, embracing all its qualities? So in some sense with similarity we recognise the totality of something. An orange is similar, but not identical, to another orange or, to a lesser degree, to a grapefruit. To see that, we don't have to divide up the qualities of the orange. We see the whole orange as similar to the other orange. But to see what's opposite to the orange we have to divide up its qualities – sweetness, juiciness, colour, shape – and then try and find qualities opposite to each of those, like sour as opposed to sweet. So with similarity we in a sense relate to wholeness, and with opposites we end up with a collection of bits. I think we might see that this difference between similarity and opposites is significant. It's as if similarity stands for unity and opposites stand for division.

Jung was quite interested in the idea of similarity and discusses the possible role of similarity in projection – although he uses the word analogy (resemblance, equivalence) instead of similarity. Jung's idea of projection is so well known now that it has entered the cultural mainstream. He states that whatever is unconscious in us, but needing to become conscious, can be projected – that is to say, seen as a quality belonging to something or someone outside ourselves. This is an important subject which I only mention here in passing. But in the following passage Jung suggests that it may be a kind of similarity that triggers the projection. There's a similarity

– or analogy – between something inside you and the thing outside you that apparently has those qualities. "Such a content is an autonomous complex divorced from consciousness, leading a life of its own in the psychic non-ego and instantly projecting itself whenever it is constellated in any way – that is, whenever attracted by something analogous to it in the outside world."[20]

Projection is ubiquitous. We see what is unconscious in ourselves in the outside world. For example, Jung was one of the first to propose that we see the contra-sexual within ourselves in an external figure. A man can see something of his own feminine qualities in a woman, and a woman can see something of her own masculine qualities in a man. These ideas are far reaching indeed. And, of course, cultural content is full of projection. What does a king or queen mean for a nation? What does a cow or a rose symbolise for a culture? And perhaps through all of this runs the idea of similarity.

Similarity also reminds us of resonance in sound, which occurs when one object is vibrating at the same natural frequency as that of a second object, producing for example the resonant sound effect between two musical instruments.

So similarity, resonance and analogy could all point to the way things connect or disconnect, or the way in which we experience connection or disconnection. Similarity and resonance seem to suggest harmony or communion or a kind of recognition between separate things as opposed to disharmony, discord or disconnection.

So far we've only considered similarity and resonance as local phenomena. There's nothing non-local about the similarity between the two oranges, or the way I see and recognise that similarity. There's nothing non-local about the way two stringed instruments resonate together. The science of light and sound waves offers enough explanation. But can we expand the notion of similarity and see its hand in synchronistic events, and perhaps in non-local effects in general?

In Jung's famous example of the scarab beetle, no progress was being made. Jung was frustrated and could see no way forward. Then help comes from an unexpected quarter. The patient dreams of a scarab beetle. A rose chafer, which is *similar* to the scarab in that it belongs to the same taxonomic family as the scarab, appears at the window, is caught by Jung and shown to the patient. The treatment, according to Jung, now progressed satisfactorily. (Of course Jung's evidence here is anecdotal. However we could perhaps remember that in his essay on synchronicity he offers it as part of a larger body of evidence, some of which is less convincing and some more, but which taken in totality constitutes a coherent argument. This is also the approach I take in the present book.)

Was the *similarity* between the inner event (the patient's dream) and the outer event (appearance of the rose chafer) a significant factor in this apparent connection between inner and outer? Could similarity play a role in synchronistic events – events which are separate in space, and sometimes in time as well, but which are nevertheless meaningfully connected? In Jung's example no one could argue that the psychic state of the patient and her dream of a scarab beetle could *cause* the appearance of a similar beetle at the consulting room window. However it may be that the different elements of the situation – Jung's frustration, the patient's condition, the dream of the scarab, the appearance of the rose chafer – came together in time and space in such a way as to produce a dynamic change in the situation. Could this coming together be an expression of similarity (or resonance) – between the patient's psychic state, the dream beetle, and the real beetle – arising in the conditions of need (the patient's) and openness or readiness (in the therapist, Jung, as well as perhaps in the unconscious of the patient)?

Jung, as we've already seen, gives quite frequent consideration to the concept of similarity. Here, in a letter to Pauli, he considers similarity as a non-local phenomenon. He writes, "synchronicity could be understood as an *ordering* system by means of which 'similar' things coincide, without there being an apparent 'cause'."[21] Could similarity be a kind of non-causal orderedness that connects apparently separate objects and events across space and time? This seems to be what Jung is suggesting.

Similarity shows up elsewhere. For example, it plays a key role in biologist Rupert Sheldrake s theories of morphic resonance and morphic fields.

According to Sheldrake, anything that shows organisation of form and function has a morphic field. For example, individual organisms from bacteria to whales are organised by specific types of morphic field known as morphogenetic fields. These are fields of influence that organise the form, growth and function of living organisms. They allow an organism to maintain its form and carry on its functioning and growth over the span of its lifetime.

Morphogenetic fields also exist in nested hierarchies or "holarchies". For example cells are organised by fields, which are part of organs organised by their own fields, which are part of a body organised by its own field. Even large group 'organisms' such as swarms, flocks and herds are also organised by these fields.

It is the effect of such an information field that allows an organism to grow and develop according to specific patterns of form and function. The field of a butterfly say, influences the growth and form of the individual butterfly, and has itself been influenced by all similar previous organisms – all previous butterflies. There would be a field for, say, the whole insect class, and within that field, more specific fields for the whole order of moths and butterflies, and yet further fields for specific butterfly families. Such fields thus consist of information which enable the structure and function of the individual butterfly to develop on every level – behaviour, physical systems, organs, cells, etc. – according to the information that constitutes the field. New adaptive behaviour in an individual butterfly will also influence the collective field of butterflies, so that a morphogenetic field, as well as its corresponding physical organisms, is itself evolving.

On this point – the evolution of morphogenetic fields – Sheldrake is emphatic. They, along with their related organisms, are to be thought of as evolving. They aren't like the fixed eternal forms existing in an ideal world proposed by Plato. They aren't Platonic forms. Rather they are information fields that evolve in tandem with their host organisms. These fields can be said to be 'eternal' in the sense that they outlive their host organisms. Individual organisms live and die, but the field in a certain sense sustains. Sheldrake believes then that such fields constitute a kind of memory.

Non-biological entities such as atoms or chemical compounds are also organised by their own classes of morphic fields. Minerals and crystals are organised by their own fields, as are planets, solar systems and galaxies. Morphic fields could also organise such entities as human societies, and even languages and behaviour.

This, in briefest outline, is Sheldrake's idea.[22] Now we come to the question of how they work. He proposes that morphogenetic fields (the class of morphic fields related to living organisms) are fields of influence that link with their "host" organisms through similar resonance (Sheldrake terms this morphic resonance). That is to say they're tuned to the organism through a rhythmic activity that is similar in both field and organism. This tuning allows information to be conveyed between field and organism. This communication, as we shall see, may not obey the laws of spacetime. It may be more like a simultaneous effect similar to that occurring between particles in quantum entanglement.

In Sheldrake's understanding there is probably no transfer of energy or signal involved in morphic resonance. Rather morphic field and organism are in a kind of resonance with each other which allows both to influence each other. Field influences organism, and organism influences field. Thus there is two-way communication between them. This communication is probably not limited by the speed of light. It doesn't operate according to the laws of the fields known to science (electromagnetic, etc.). Rather it could be based on the similar rhythmic activity (i.e. the rhythmic activity of a dynamic pattern with mathematical or geometric properties) of field and organism, and constitutes a resonance that produces a kind of instantaneous communication or knowing.

He writes, "We are used to the idea of causal influences acting at a distance in space and time through fields: for example, when we look at distant stars we are subject to influences coming from far away and from thousands of years ago through the medium of the electromagnetic field in which the light is travelling. But the idea of morphic resonance involves a different kind of action at a distance, which is harder to conceive of because it does not involve the movement of quanta of energy through any of the known fields of physics."[23]

Thus "morphic resonance involves a kind of action at a distance in both space and time. The hypothesis assumes that this influence does not decline with distance in space and time."[24]

In other words these influences aren't bound by the laws of spacetime, as are the influences propagated through electromagnetic fields. Further, "In considering the effects of morphic resonance over astronomical distances the question of how fast its influence can travel inevitably arises. There are at least three possibilities. Either this influence propagates at its own characteristic speed, which might be greater or less than the speed of light. Or it propagates at the speed of light. *Or its effects may be in some way be analogous to the non-local correlations in quantum theory, which are in a sense instantaneous* (emphasis mine). There seems at present no basis for deciding between these possibilities."[25]

Such an information field could be constituted of a kind of dynamic pattern which may only be possible to understand through mathematics and geometry, just as the laws of physics can only be understood through mathematical equations. (The philosophers of the ancient world also attempted to formulate their understanding of reality through number and geometry.) Morphic fields may thus be best conceived of as ordering fields which operate according to mathematical laws and relationships. Such mathematical or geometrical patterns become apparent to our senses in the ordered dynamic patterns found in the physical universe – for example in atomic configurations, crystal formation, or geometric patterns seen in flowering plants. At one time music was also understood to be an expression of these laws or relationships.

It seems possible then that the "purposeful" non-local correlations occurring in both synchronicity and morphic resonance could be facilitated by the principle of similarity.

In another realm of inquiry, physicist David Bohm proposes similarity as a possible underlying principle of reality. Bohm has proposed the existence of an underlying unity behind the world of apparently separate objects and events. He names this unity the "implicate order", and the world that we experience, and which arises from the implicate order, the "explicate order" (see chapter 7). However the implicate order, as well as being an undivided totality contains, as it were, in potential, all possible differences. Thus Bohm states: The implicate order can be thought of as a ground beyond time, a totality, out of which each moment is projected into the explicate order."[26]

In discussing Bohm's work, Sheldrake writes: "The implicate order is a realm in which all things and events are enfolded in a total wholeness and unity, which as it were underlies the explicate order of the world we experience through our senses."[27]

It may be that here too similarity has a role. Describing the unified field behind the world of separate objects and events that we normally experience, Bohm says: "Moreover such a field would not be located anywhere. When it projects back into the totality (the implicate order), since no space and time are relevant there, all things of a similar nature might get connected together or resonate in totality."[28]

All things of a similar nature might get connected together or resonate in totality. It seems then that things that are similar in their form or function, as well as in resonance, could somehow know each other, awaken each other, activate each other, across space and time – no matter what distance is involved – and perhaps even no matter how far they're separated in time. Such relationships are thus not ones of cause and effect, but rather they are connections sustained by a kind of resonance based on similarity. This resonance, in which no signal transfer is involved, could then represent a kind of recognition or memory of oneness. It could, as it were, be an expression of this background unity. As we shall see, there is no essential separation in the implicate order. Thus any knowing, awareness or perception sustained in one separate part (an individual organism for example) wouldn't only exist in that part. It could exist in the whole as well. It could somehow be the property of the whole. Furthermore, because the whole also contains all possible separate parts, each part still, in some manner, carries the possibility or the trace of the total knowing of the whole. That total knowing could somehow be awoken when two things (existing as separate objects or events in spacetime) resonate together in similarity. In the human experience of events and things that are linked in the absence of any apparent causal connections – such as in synchronicity, in different kinds of precognition, or in divinatory methods such as the *I Ching* (see chapter 8) – this awakening of the whole in the individual part (our individual self) can be felt by us as an experience of insight, self-knowledge or healing.

The idea of similarity is also significant in the history of medicine and healing. It's the cornerstone of homeopathic theory and practice. Let's take a look at the place of similarity in homeopathy, and as we do so inquire further into the way non-locality might show up in our world and in our experience.[29]

5. Similar Resonance in Healing

The idea that a medical or healing approach could be based on the principle of similarity isn't new. Paracelsus, sometimes considered the father of modern medicine, was serious about the use of similarity in medicine. And hints can be found that there may have been an understanding of similarity in healing and medicine long before the modern era.[30] It may be that the medical approach that we know today as homeopathy is the latest link in a chain stretching back hundreds or even thousands of years.

Homeopathy is based on similarity, or the *law of similars* as it's known. In homeopathy the law of similars states that a substance that can produce a pattern of disturbance of function and sensation in a healthy person (i.e. can cause symptoms) can, when given in a suitable dose, cure the same pattern of disturbance in the sick person. This is why Samuel Hahnemann (the founder of homeopathy) called it *homœopathy* (the correct spelling taken from the original Greek), meaning 'like suffering'. The law of similars has been arrived at through hypothesis and experimental observation, in just the same way that modern scientific laws and hypotheses are established.

Homeopathic procedure depends on the ability to assess the degree of similarity between a remedial substance and a person's state of health. How to do this is the subject of homeopathic philosophy and methodology. The prerequisite for homeopathic procedure is the testing of specially prepared substances on healthy human test subjects. Researchers record and establish how a particular substance (usually from a plant, mineral or animal source) that has been prepared in the form of a special non-toxic dose can influence the health and well-being of a test subject. This experiment gives the basic data about which symptoms a particular homeopathic substance (a substance converted into a medicinal agent through homeopathic preparation) can cause in a healthy test subject. (These homeopathic trials are traditionally called homeopathic provings). This in turn becomes the data that helps the homeopath to establish which remedial substance is most similar to a person's state of illness and suffering. This illness or suffering of the individual is described to a homeopath in terms of the individual's own experience of their illness. The patient describes what is wrong in terms of altered functions (dysfunction) as well as troublesome sensations and feelings. This is exactly what test subjects had already done when under the influence of test substances. The test subject under the influence of a test substance describes their experience in terms of altered functions (the derangement of the psychological and/or physical system) and of altered sensations (the inner experience of those derangements or dysfunctions).

Homeopathic remedies are prepared using a method of serial dilution and intermittent shaking up of the diluting medium. These dilutions can be taken far beyond the point at which there is any chance of finding any trace at all of the original solute. Hence from the perspective of the current scientific paradigm homeopathic remedies can't possibly work. It is maintained that any beneficial effect must be due to the placebo effect. The prevailing scientific view is that homeopathy could only be accepted as a valid therapeutic system if a local, cause-and-effect mechanism can be demonstrated. In science the idea of locality explains phenomena as being connected one with another through measurable cause-and-effect relationships. Examples of this are one ball striking another producing a change of trajectory, or light waves emitted from a source travelling via an electromagnetic field and striking the retina of the eye, or a biological compound such as a hormone producing physiological changes in the body. In the absence of any remaining material in the homeopathic dilution, the only other viable local explanation is "memory-in-water" – the capacity of water to retain electromagnetic information even after any physical trace of the solute has disappeared from the dilution.

Contemporary science explains all physical phenomena in terms of local, cause-and-effect actions and reactions. There is considerable research, and some robust evidence that memory-in-water could provide a local causative explanation for the action of homeopathic remedies. There is some good evidence to suggest that water containing a substance in solution, which has undergone serial dilutions to the point at which there is no trace of the original solute, can still retain electromagnetic charges and structural changes as though the original solute was still present.

A number of questions arise from the memory-in-water hypothesis, which make the argument for memory-in-water as the sole basis for the mechanism of action of homeopathic remedies inconclusive. For example, in a homeopathic preparation how does the water 'know' to retain the electromagnetic or structural trace of only the intended diluted substance (the homeopathic remedy)? What about other 'stray' substances that might come from the environment (such as fungal spores) or from the experimental equipment (such as impurities leached from glass vials)? How would the water select for only the designated substance? And what about the previous life of the water in which many other solutes could have left their mark in the water?

Another question arises from research suggesting that water can have its structure changed through the effect of thoughts and intentions. If this turned out to be true it would mean water was being structurally changed in the absence of any solute or of any electromagnetic influence. If water was being changed through thought and intention, any such activity would have to be non-local, just like telepathy for example.

Is it possible that thought and intention plays a part in some, if not all, memory-in-water phenomena? If this were true then it would indeed remind us of the situation in quantum mechanics where the manner of observation has a bearing on experimental outcomes. The "entire experimental setup" has to be taken into account (the observed, the observer, experimental equipment and so on). Nothing can be excluded from the total experimental situation.[31]

With this in mind, it is not so far-fetched to think of the action of homeopathic remedies in terms of non-local connections, as we find in phenomena such as quantum entanglement or synchronicity. This approach does not rule out the memory-in-water hypothesis. The evidence that electromagnetic effects or structural changes can be retained by water cannot be ignored. But in the view posited here, the laws governing memory-in-water would be understood in the context of a higher order non-local reality appearing in such phenomena as synchronicity and morphic resonance. And possibly in homeopathy too.

If homeopathy does act through a non-local instantaneous connection mediated by similarity, then this connection could be a kind of resonance between morphic fields. The fields themselves wouldn't be limited by space and time. So the connection could occur across space. It could also occur across time.

Could such a field – the morphic field of a substance that has been transformed into a homeopathic preparation – somehow resonate through similarity with the morphic field of a particular person? A link of similarity could be established between remedial substance and suffering individual. Or the morphic field of a proving event itself (one that took place at some time in the past) could resonate with the field of the individual in need of help. Such a field would involve the morphic field of a remedial substance, as well as the collective field of all the individuals involved. In fact such a field would include the whole experimental setup" of the proving. That is to say it would include the substance, the individuals involved, as well as all the physical, emotional, psychological and spiritual experiences of trial subjects (provers) during the proving. It would also include synchronistic events that occurred during – or even before and after – the trial period. Because such a field wouldn't be limited in time, it would also include all cultural associations as well as scientific knowledge that had accrued over time in relation to a particular substance.

Of course any such resonance of fields might need some kind of mechanism in order to result in a physical mode of activity. Memory-in-water could be involved in such a mechanism. But we need to remember that water seems to be capable of retaining local effects, as well as non-local effects such as those of thought and intention.

Such potential connection between fields might also need very specific modes of attention and intention in order to be activated. This reminds us of the conditions necessary, according to Jung, for synchronistic occurrences. The attention and intention present in the homeopathic consultation could activate the power of similarity. To put it another way, we might say that everyone in the consultation setup (experimental setup) partakes in the morphic field or morphic pattern of which the healing substance is also a part. Both homeopath and patient become part of the pattern. So everyone is involved here. The patient with her story and description of symptoms; the homeopath who listens, observes and records; the homeopath's research and seeking for the most similar remedy. All these factors somehow activate and become part of a morphic pattern which itself isn't restricted to any location in space or time. In a sense this pattern is potentially everywhere in space as well as being unlimited in time – that is timeless. Such a morphic pattern can include subjective and objective events (events I experience as in here or out there) happening anywhere in space and at any time (including the future).

Without the idea of similarity none of this makes any sense. Without similarity not much will happen. Any healing activity that does occur will be due to (the not inconsiderable) placebo effect. It is the power of similarity activated through all the channels I've described that distinguishes homeopathic activity from placebo activity. For homeopathic similarity to be activated a number of key factors must be present. There has to be a remedial substance and there has to be some kind of recorded knowledge of that substance – through provings; through scientific knowledge; through cultural and symbolic associations. There also has to be the work of both patient and homeopath to come to understand which pattern – a morphic pattern usually connected with a natural substance – is active in the patient and lies behind her symptoms and troublesome sensations. But this understanding and subsequent selection has to be very specific. It has to be very similar for a homeopathic remedy to work. Without a high degree of similarity between the known symptoms of a remedial substance and the symptoms displayed by a suffering person, homeopathic remedies don't work. Low-level similarity means low-level results. High-level similarity means high-level results. And this is just one of several factors that distinguish homeopathic action from placebo action.

Memory-in-water, in as much as it can be shown to be a sustainable hypothesis – might turn out to be an epiphenomenon of a higher order non-local resonance. Thus it would not be the primary mechanism of action for homeopathic remedies. Memory-in-water might be like a focus or a bridge in the larger phenomenon of non-local connections working through similarity.

This argument might also remind us of the paradox found at the heart of quantum mechanics. In this paradox, matter takes on particular properties such as measurable spin, location or momentum only when an observation or measurement is made. Until then matter exists in an undefined superpositional state. That means something takes on specific form and values out of a superpositional and non-specific state. This is a process in which, so to speak, "no-thing" becomes "some-thing." Or potential becomes actual.

We might also say that in the homeopathic healing process potential becomes actual. It is as though the process of homeopathic potentisation (which includes the capacity of water for memory-in-water) mimics the quantum mechanical process in reverse. The particular (in this case the natural substance) is, as it were, returned to its superpositional state. Then in the process of the homeopathic consultation, followed by remedy selection and prescription, healing potential that is in some sense superpositional is collapsed into actual healing power with the capacity to alter sensations and functions in the minds and bodies of real human beings. The homeopathic process is the fundamental act of making potential (the superpositional) actual. And, just as in quantum mechanics, the presence of observers, experimenters and experimental apparatus (laboratory equipment) cannot be excluded from the whole homeopathic setup.

For all this to happen there has to be enough similarity between the remedial substance and the pattern of ill health in a suffering individual. Homeopathic healing depends on the ability of the homeopath to match the symptom picture displayed by the patient to a known symptom picture displayed by a test subject or group of test subjects in a homeopathic proving. This is the basis of homeopathic work. Of course, there is much more to be said concerning homeopathic procedure and how homeopaths go about the business of making homeopathic prescriptions. This has been written about extensively elsewhere by many others, including myself.[32]

Similarity as awakener

The access to a morphic field pattern associated with a particular mineral, plant or animal substance can bring about a healing response in the individual. Through the agency of the similarity between the symptoms of dysfunction in a patient and the symptoms of dysfunction produced by a specific substance in a test subject in a homeopathic remedy trial, a healing reaction takes place in the patient. But since no substance is involved here it's possible that the beneficial changes are initiated through a kind of information transfer or instantaneous connection or instantaneous recognition between morphic fields associated with the substance and with the suffering individual.

Local mechanisms such as memory-in-water that might be involved in, or in some way activated by, this information connection or this similarity resonance, that lead to beneficial restoration of function and sense of well-being in a patient, are only beginning to be understood. Obviously no substance is involved. It is however possible that memory-in-water could be involved in any such mechanism. Water, which seems to be shown to have highly plastic characteristics, could be a kind of bridge or interface between the world of non-local instantaneous connections and the world of local cause-and-effect relationships.

Is it possible that similarity, in connecting things that resonate together simultaneously, across space and time, facilitates or awakens some kind of innate knowing? Could it somehow 'enlighten' the situation, and in that spread of previously inaccessible 'information', insight, liberation from stuckness and healing are made possible? When, in synchronicity, or quantum entanglement, or in homeopathy, objects or events are connected and are influencing each other, they are not doing so through local cause-and-effect reactions. Rather such separate phenomena could be connected through similarity. And I suggest that in being connected through similarity they somehow 'remind' each other of the unity behind everything and out of which all apparently separate objects and events arise.

And what could this signify, to be reminded of this unity? Non-local connections suggest that behind the world of appearances there is no separation. There is only one, only an unbroken totality. It is possible that to know this is to know the truth and thus to experience an influx of truth, meaning and healing. Perhaps this knowing – that there is no separation, only one – is ultimately the source of wisdom and healing. This knowing, this connection, could facilitate the release of healing power in homeopathic treatment and it could also trigger the spontaneous experience of enlightenment or awakening or release from suffering reported by individuals, some with a spiritual heritage and others with none, throughout history and from all places and cultures

So let's continue with the idea of a oneness world and a twoness world, and, in passing, also introduce the idea of quantum coherence.

6. Quantum Body

Oneness world is a totality beyond division, and therefore also beyond description, even by such a term as oneness (more on this later). By twoness world I mean the apparent world of cause and effect. The twoness world is one of objects and wave-propagating fields that affect one another in spacetime. The ruling principle in this world is the speed of light. One could say that light, and thus the speed of light, is a prerequisite for experiencing a world of separate objects in interaction with one another. Physical light and our seeing of the world are closely bound up with our rational capacity to name and classify things. Light and time are also bound together. Go beyond the speed of light and you are in a sense beyond time.

It seems obvious that only things that are separate one from another can be in cause-and-effect relationships with each other or can be linked together through action and reaction. We can imagine for example two balls colliding with each other. They're in a cause-and-effect relationship with each other. The motion of one ball produces a result, the motion of the other ball. But we can't imagine a single ball in a cause-and-effect relationship with itself (although in the quantum world a quantum object can interfere with itself). Or we can think of the cause-and-effect relationship of sound waves transmitted from a source, producing vibrations in the middle ear. But what about the commonly reported incidence of knowing that something will happen before it happens? In this case no cause-and-effect relationship between the two events (the knowing and the event) can be demonstrated. (Of course more research always needs to be done to show that such examples of precognition are statistically more common than coincidence would allow.)

Despite major advances in genetics, genetic engineering and biotechnology, twoness-world thinking still permeates modern biology and medicine. This means that many modern biologists, rooted in the world view of classical physics, still consider a system such as the human body to be an array of immensely complex cause-and-effect relationships between separate units and systems such as DNA, proteins, hormones, cells, nervous system and brain. But it may be that such a system, with millions of perfectly coordinated processes, cannot be wholly explained in terms of interlinked cause-and-effect reactions. It may be that non-locality, as demonstrated in quantum entanglement, as well as in synchronicity, is at work right here in our physical presence allowing our bodies to function as an expression of countless perfectly coordinated events.

Quantum biology is a field of scientific inquiry that has gradually emerged over the last 100 years, and dates back to initial suggestions by Niels Bohr that the laws of quantum mechanics could play a significant role in biological systems. The development of this field was paused with the discovery of DNA and advances in genetics which the scientists of the day believed provided all the explanation needed for the fundamentals of biological functioning. There has been a gradual resurgence of interest in this field.[33]

Geneticist Mae-Wan Ho suggests that entanglement could operate at much larger scales than is currently understood. If this is the case it could help to understand how it's possible for the millions of processes found in a living organism such as the human body to be perfectly synchronised in a manner impossible to imagine if we view the body as only functioning through time-bound cause-and-effect processes such as the hormonal or neural signalling between different parts.

She writes: "A coherent space-time structure theoretically enables 'instantaneous' communication to occur over a range of time scales and spatial extents."[34] She continues: "Living organisms depend on quantum reactions, not only in the sense that quantum tunnelling is explicitly recognised in electron and proton transfer, but especially in the sense that all energy transductions are carried out by individual enzymes and other molecules acting as 'quantum energy machines' in which individual quanta of energy released are directly transferred from the point of release to the point of use. The coordination of such activities requires nothing short of quantum coherence, especially in view of the rapidity and specificity with which responses or intercommunication can take place in the living system."[35] (Quantum tunnelling is another observed yet unexplained phenomenon in physics. It appears that a particle which doesn't have enough energy to get past an energy barrier can nevertheless appear on the other side of the barrier, having apparently passed through the barrier. This is known as quantum tunnelling. It isn't known how fast this change in location happens. But one possibility is that the particle 'teleports' instantaneously. If this is so, it, like quantum entanglement, defies the principle of spacetime causality. It has even been hypothesised that a particle could be found on the other side of the barrier *before* it has left its original location.)

For me the inference is as follows. The apparently separate parts and systems of living organisms, while sustaining cause-and-effect relationships with each other, are also held in a 'field' of instantaneous connections which aren't regulated by spacetime, and don't obey the spacetime law of the speed of light. We can propose then that living organisms, such as our bodies, are not only defined by the twoness world, by spacetime. The human body (together with all organisms) might consist of processes and dynamics that are local and causal as well as non-local and instantaneous. Here separate systems, events and processes might be linked in a kind of unity. We could think of this as a field where, so to speak, oneness and twoness, the undivided and the divided, interpenetrate. I've termed this the intermediary world.

7. Oneness World and Twoness World

Now we come to the *oneness world*. This is harder to describe because the rational mind, which I'm using now to write these words, itself works in the mode of twoness. It distinguishes one object from another, compares things, and above all separates the subject from the object. In as much as my mind separates, analyses, and classifies, it exists in the world of twoness, of duality, of polarity. We could even say that the very basis for our experience of twoness is the fact that we see what's out there as different from ourselves.

The oneness world isn't made of separate things. It exists as one, as *one without another*. Being one, there can be no separation, and thus no cause and effect, and no action and reaction. It is whole and unbroken. This world isn't directly known in physics. It's not known, but is suspected. That's why there's a search for a universal field or wave that underlies and unifies all phenomena.

Einstein, although he believed in an objectively existing reality following its own laws independent of the presence of an observer, also believed in the possibility of a unified and unbroken wholeness underlying reality. "Einstein did in fact very seriously try to obtain such a description in terms of a unified field theory. He took the total field of the whole universe as a primary description. This field is continuous and indivisible. Particles are then to be regarded as certain kinds of abstraction from the total field, corresponding to regions of very intense field (called singularities)."[36]

David Bohm himself posited the presence of an unbroken wholeness as the basis of the world we experience via our senses. He named this the *holomovement*. "To generalize so as to emphasize undivided wholeness, we shall say that what 'carries' an implicate order is the *holomovement*, which is an unbroken and undivided totality. In certain cases, we can abstract particular aspects of the holomovement (e.g., light, electrons, sound, etc.), but more generally, all forms of the holomovement merge and are inseparable. Thus, in its totality, the holomovement is not limited in any specifiable way at all. It is not required to conform to any particular order, or to be bounded by any particular measure. Thus, *the holomovement is undefineable and immeasurable*."[37] (In his model there are actually three elements. First the holomovement which is whole and unbroken. Then the implicate order, which is whole and unbroken but somehow has the capacity to give rise to all particularities and differences. Then the explicate order – the order of all apparently separate and more or less stable forms. These forms are 'projections' into the spacetime world emanating, so to speak, from the implicate order. For all practical purposes we only need consider the implicate and explicate orders – the undivided totality and the world of apparent differences.)

Whether we refer to this unbroken wholeness as a unified field, the holomovement or the implicate order, if such a unity lies at the basis of all experienced reality, it must include any observer or any form of consciousness capable of perceiving. Because it is stated that it's a unity, unbroken, containing no separate bits, this also means that any observing consciousness cannot be a separate consciousness. Since there is no separation, anything that is aware and able to experience, must at the same time, in some way, be the whole, the totality. Our discriminating minds simply can't perceive this directly because of an intrinsic sense of separation.

There's more to this. We can perhaps think about the reality of an unbroken wholeness described above. But it's almost impossible to conceive of an unbroken whole that also contains all possible separate entities. But this is exactly what Bohm proposes in his theory of the implicate order. All possibilities exist there, unlimited by spacetime, and yet able to have a spacetime existence. It is as though the whole was composed of an infinite number of possibilities, and that the whole, under the right conditions, could 'collapse' into or manifest as any one of those possibilities in spacetime.

However, any object or event existing in spacetime (twoness) still remains as a 'collapsed' or specified version of the whole (collapsed: so called after the collapse of the wave function, the term used in quantum physics to describe how, at the level of the very small, things only take on specific values in the act of being measured). When something becomes specific, it remains, at the same time, the whole unbroken unity. Thus all apparently separate objects and events are at the same time still the whole. In this view of reality, any separate bit or event can potentially be in instantaneous knowing with any other bit or event. Why? Because all separate bits are still the whole, and there can be, in reality, no separation between apparently separate bits. This, it seems to me, is the inevitable conclusion arising from these considerations.

"Thus we come to a new general physical description in which 'everything implicates everything' in an order of undivided wholeness."[38]

Are the understandings arising from the work of 20th-century physicists essentially new? In the world's wisdom traditions, such as Advaita Vedanta, it's said that there's a oneness behind everything, a unity behind all apparently separate objects and events. It's also said that this unity cannot be known directly (as an object) because it is not an object of consciousness. It is consciousness itself. It is the subject without an object. It can only really be sensed or directly experienced as presence. And the sense of presence is not an object of consciousness. Rather, it is a quality of consciousness itself.

Of course, the understandings that have arisen for 20th-century physicists, and those that arose for the Vedic sages of the past, have come about through entirely different approaches. For the physicists the outer world has been the object of their scrutiny and enquiry. This scientific enquiry into the nature of outer reality is primarily a mental operation embedded in a quest for knowledge and understanding. This process, along with any resulting hypotheses about the nature of physical reality, is orientated towards, and needs confirmation by, enquiry through the senses (including the technology that extends the senses such as radio telescopes, electron microscopes, magnetic resonance imaging devices and so on). On the other hand, the sages of the past belonged to traditions of contemplation and reflection. As well as observing the outer world, they observed their inner world, their inner experience, in great detail and depth.

Nevertheless the groundbreaking physicists of the first half of the 20th century – Bohr, Heisenberg and others – seemed to be moving towards a similar understanding as that achieved by the contemplatives of the past. It's possible that the examination of the outer world has led, and continues to lead, to a similar model of reality as that posited by the sages of the past.

This brings us to the question of the relationship between the oneness world and the twoness world. But in attempting to address this question we immediately run into a problem. If there is only unity, only unbroken wholeness, how can we talk of a relationship between a oneness world and a twoness world? How can we even talk of twoness at all? So before going any further we have to remind ourselves that any such notion of a oneness world and twoness world can, in an unbroken reality, only exist in our conceptual minds. In the ultimate reality, described, for example, in Advaita Vedanta, there can be no such distinction, no such separation. There can only be the unity. And yet quantum theorists such as Bohm also point to the possibility that an underlying unbroken field (implicate order) would contain within it all possible particularities and differences. This is the mystery and the paradox. But, for practical purposes, and because we live and function in a world of apparently separate objects, and even because we sense and long for unity, it's still helpful to consider both oneness and twoness.

One further point. Because people think and operate in a world of duality, they have naturally thought of the two worlds, the two realities, as separate, as for example in heaven above and earth below. It's natural for us to think like this, dualistically, even though this isn't how things are in reality. For practical purposes we separate the one into two realities. But even if we do this we can still think of oneness absolutely permeating twoness. They occupy exactly the same space, so to speak. From this perspective, oneness is ever-present, permeating twoness. We just don't perceive the primary reality (oneness world) when we're operating in normal consciousness.

However oneness can, as it were, poke through into twoness in any place and at any time – as in the occurrence of events that are meaningfully linked with each other, and yet cannot be shown to be causally linked. So we could say that as we experience the everyday world, oneness is right here, right now – not somewhere else.

Staying with the notion of one thing permeating another, let's return to the idea of the implicate order. Bohm's map postulates the holomovement, the implicate order and the explicate order. The explicate order is the spacetime world of interconnected objects and events. The holomovement is the unbroken flow at the base of everything. The implicate order is also whole and unbroken, unconstrained by spacetime. However it also contains all possible differences, all possible objects and events, in potential, within itself. Another way of putting this is to say that all possible potentials for objects and events, or all possible information fields (morphic fields) coexist simultaneously in oneness. They coexist as the implicate order.

This suggests that the oneness world has the extraordinary property of 'collapsing' itself into any one particular information field, and thus one particular object or event in spacetime. But here's the important point. As oneness does this it is still the totality, still the oneness. And the thing it becomes is still the oneness. All possibilities coexist. An apparent part is still the one. The oneness world can never lose its property of oneness. Anything apparently separate is actually still the oneness, the unbroken totality.

In following this line of thought, we could say that any particular separate bit – photon, electron, atom, cell, person – can be in simultaneous connection, or in simultaneous knowing, with another separate bit. In reality those separate bits never fell out of oneness. Oneness can take on a particular potential (implicate order) and become a separate thing, or inter-woven relationship of things (explicate order) without losing its oneness. It is as though oneness were a perfect mirror (or endless emptiness which somehow endlessly mirrors) in which any apparently separate thing appears, becomes itself, sees itself, and thus finds itself.

In that act oneness appears as the particular thing in a given time and place. But that thing – an electron, an atom, you, me – is actually the oneness. Being such it has the possibility to be in instantaneous connection or knowing with any other thing.

In summary then, let us say that it's possible that no-thing can become some-thing. But as this happens, the no-thing and the some-thing remain identical. In reality these two are not different at all. They only seem so.

Platonic sphere as symbol

If you find it helpful to visualise things, then this next section may be useful. But you can also skip this part if you want to.

To think about a reality in which separate events can be connected through cause-and-effect relationships as well as having an inner connection through the principles of synchronicity and similarity, I turn to Plato for help. Plato showed (in his dialogue *Timaeus*) that there are only five ways to divide the surface of a sphere in which every face is the same and equal, and in which all lines are equal and all nodes the same. These are the *platonic solids.*

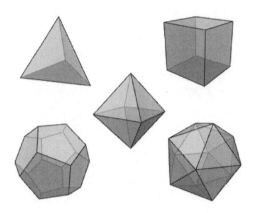

The 5 Platonic Solids

tetrahedron: 4 equal triangular faces ~ cube: 6 equal square faces
octahedron: 8 equal triangular faces
dodecahedron: 12 equal pentagonal faces ~ icosahedron: 20 equal triangular faces

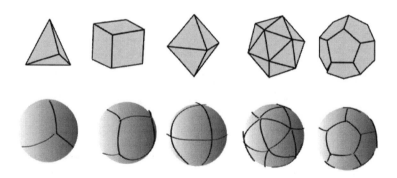

The 5 Platonic Solids shown as solids (top row) and as subdivisions
of the surface of a sphere (second row)

In the top row each node of the solid (the point where lines and planes meet) lies on the surface of an imaginary sphere enclosing the solid, and is connected to the other points by straight lines. In the second row it's the same – each point lies on the surface of the sphere, but the connecting lines follow the curve of the sphere. There you can see the solids more clearly for what they are – subdivisions of the surface of a sphere where all the subdivisions are equal.

Sphere

One triangle of a Platonic sphere, showing the nodes on the sphere's surface joined by lines that follow the curve of the sphere.

Icosahedron as a solid

Icosahedron as subdivision of a sphere (shown in 3D). The Platonic sphere (icosahedron) as an image of wholeness which also allows us to imagine the relationship of parts to the whole.

Let the sphere represent unbroken wholeness – something complete and undivided. In mystical traditions this is understood as the undivided consciousness or space that is the 'ground' of everything that appears (the apparently separate objects and events of our experience).

David Bohm describes this reality from the point of view of a physicist. He emphasises the underlying wholeness: "Thus, the 'object' is an abstraction of a relatively invariant form." [*i.e. what appears to us as an object sustaining its form through time.*] "That is to say, it is more like a pattern of movement than like a solid separate thing that exists autonomously and permanently." He continues: "Rather, we have to regard the universe as *an undivided and unbroken whole*. Division into particles, or into particles and fields, is only a crude abstraction and approximation. Thus we come to an order that is radically different from that of Galileo and Newton – the order of *undivided wholeness*."[39]

In this image the sphere itself represents this underlying unbroken wholeness. As Bohm suggests, we can't think of this as a "thing", but more like a dynamic state in which all movement, all fields and all objects exist in potential. All difference is there in the oneness.

So what about the points on the surface of the sphere? In this image they are things or events in spacetime. They represent what we see and understand as separate object/events.

In the twoness world apparently separate things are in relationships of cause and effect with each other. This is the world of classical physics which studies objects and fields within spacetime. In this image these relationships between things (points on the surface of the sphere) are represented by the connecting lines. You could say the lines represent the signals propagated via fields through which different objects in different regions of space affect each other.

But the different points on the surface of the sphere aren't only connected through 'lines' of cause and effect. They're also related through being part of the sphere – i.e. the underlying unity. This is where things get difficult because we're trying to understand a reality in which there is absolute unity, absolute oneness, but in which, at the same time, all separate things and possibilities also exist. Physicists such as Nick Herbert have wrestled with this problem:

"Non-local influences, if they existed, would not be mediated by fields or anything else. When A connects to B non-locally, nothing crosses the intervening space, hence no amount of interposed matter can shield this interaction.

Non-local influences do not diminish with distance. They are as potent at a million miles as at a millimetre.

Non-local influences act instantaneously. The speed of their transmission is not limited by the velocity of light.

A non-local interaction links up one location with another without crossing space, without decay, and without delay. A non-local interaction is, in short, *unmediated*, *unmitigated*, and *immediate*.

Despite physicists' traditional rejection of non-local interactions, despite the fact that all known forces are incontestably local, despite Einstein's prohibition against superluminal [*faster than light*] connections, and despite the fact that no experiment has ever shown a single case of unmediated faster-than-light communication, Bell maintains that the world is filled with innumerable non-local influences. Furthermore these unmediated connections are present not only in rare and exotic circumstances, but underlie all the events of everyday life. Non-local connections are ubiquitous because reality itself is non-local.

Not all physicists believe Bell's proof to be an airtight demonstration of the necessary existence of non-local connections. But the alternative these critics offer instead seem to me to be generally obscure and/or preposterous. As we shall see… some physicists will go so far as to actually 'deny reality itself' rather than accept Bell's audacious conclusion that quantum reality must be non-local."[40]

Therefore: "A universe that displays *local phenomena* built upon a *non-local reality* is the only sort of world consistent with known facts and Bell's proof."[41]

In a sense then, it's possible that everything is entangled with everything else. This doesn't mean that everything is in a merged soup. It means that every separate thing as it emerges from the underlying unity (implicate becoming explicate) becomes a unique thing which is at once separate but at the same time the complete unity. Perhaps this is why spiritual traditions have used the diamond, or similar precious stone, as a symbol. In the cut diamond we see difference and unity as aspects of the same thing – many facets reflecting one light.

In this view of reality, the totality, the cosmos, is somehow contained in each separate part. Each thing, each atom, cell, organism, planet, galaxy is at the same time the whole, the all. "Rather, a *total order* is contained, in some *implicit* sense, in each region of space and time…So we may be led to explore the notion that in some sense each region contains a total structure 'enfolded' within it."[42]

Returning to the image of the sphere as a model of reality we can say that although separate things can be in causal relationships of action and reaction with each other (symbolised by the points on the surface of the sphere joined by lines), they can also be in a state of union with each other, in which paradoxically there isn't really any 'each other'. Thus potentially any 'one' can be in immediate knowing and communication with any 'other'. In the symbolism of the sphere, points on the sphere have surface (cause-and-effect) connections, as well as the property of being part of the whole sphere itself.

In the next chapter we approach the intermediary world from the perspective of traditional Taoist philosophy.

8. Intermediary World

The idea that behind the world of appearances there are forces (in earlier times understood as powers, beings, gods, goddesses and so on) that invisibly shape our lives and activities for good or ill is, or was, universal.

In some traditions it's understood and felt to be an all-pervading reality or unity that underlies everything. The unity underpinning everything, like the holomovement already discussed, has been referred to as God, the Tao, heaven, the void and great spirit. Through ritual and prayer people have always sought to call on this underlying presence for sustenance, guidance and healing. We could even go so far as to say that calling on the world behind appearances, whether understood as an array of powers and beings or as a single presence or reality, through ritual and prayer has been the central preoccupation of the many cultures that preceded our own. (The different powers, beings or qualities may actually be thought of as qualities or facets of the unity that underlies all appearances.) This brings us to a consideration of the intermediary world.

When a priest in a Christian church blesses the bread and wine (s)he's acting as an intermediary. When a devotee pours milk over the lingam in a Hindu temple (s)he's acting as an intermediary in the intermediary world. The shaman in traditional cultures was (and still is) acting as an intermediary. (S)he facilitates healing and guidance from the world beyond appearances, the oneness world. Creating and employing methods by which the oneness world can appear in the twoness world is understood here as the business of the intermediary world. The practices of calling upon the oneness world are what constitute the intermediary world. We could also say that those who conduct the rituals and prayers which seek an opening to the oneness world, and even to further the appearance of oneness in twoness, are the intermediaries.

Many of us, conditioned as we are by a postmodern and materialistic view of the world might easily believe that the results of ritual and prayer are at most rather general and non-specific, and at the least simply imagined, and not real at all. But is it possible that the activity of ritual which seeks to bring the oneness world into the twoness world could also produce concrete and practical results?

The use of the *I Ching*, the ancient Chinese oracular text, is a good example of such a ritual – a methodology that in connecting our spacetime existence to a larger presence or pattern produces definite and practical results.

The *I Ching*, or Book of Changes, grew out of a profound understanding of the forces at work in nature, the cosmos and in the life of individual and culture. It held a central place in Chinese spiritual life, culture and political life for hundreds, if not thousands, of years.

Chinese philosophers of the past understood the lives of nature, of individuals, of culture and of cosmos as the interplay of two fundamental forces at work in all phenomena, in all the interweaving of events in spacetime. These are called Yang and Yin.

Yang is represented by an unbroken line:

_____

Yin is represented by a broken line:

_____   _____

In the various translations of the *I Ching* that appeared in the West in the 20th century the yang unbroken line is generally understood to be firm, strong, dynamic and active (often thought of as characteristics of the archetypal male principle). The yin broken line is thought of as being passive, responsive, flexible, adaptable and yielding (often thought of as characteristics of the archetypal female principle). All phenomena are understood to be expressions of varying combinations of yin and yang moving in dynamic cycles. The qualities of yin and yang as they occur in nature are extensively elaborated in practical applications of Chinese philosophy such as the *I Ching* or the therapeutic system of acupuncture. Some examples of the classification of yang and yin in nature are man and woman, mountain and valley, sun and moon, light and shadow or hot and dry in contrast to cold and damp. Your individual life can also be seen in terms of the interplay and circulation of the two primary forces of yin and yang.

In the random casting of special coins or yarrow stalks, these two different lines, the yin and the yang, are combined together in a series of six lines to give 64 possible arrangements or hexagrams (there are a total of 64 combinations of yang and yin lines when arranged in groups of six lines). For example Hexagram 1, called *The Creative,* is made up of six unbroken yang lines, and Hexagram 2, known as *The Receptive,* is made up of six broken yin lines.

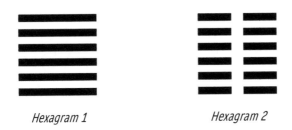

Hexagram 1   Hexagram 2

Any individual line can also be a so-called moving line. That is a line which is in the process of yang becoming yin or yin becoming yang. Any particular line can be about to become its opposite. This means that any particular hexagram can transform into a different one. This gives a more comprehensive reading where both hexagrams are consulted, and special attention is also given to any moving lines (there could be anywhere between no moving lines and six moving lines in a particular hexagram). The fall of the coins or sticks determines the makeup of the hexagram. The casting also determines whether any particular line is simply a yin or yang line, or whether it's a moving line. For example, if you cast hexagram 1, *The Creative,* where the top two lines are moving (the top two yang lines are changing into their opposites, two yin lines) you would have the following arrangement:

Hexagram 1 changing to Hexagram 34

For your answer you would look at the images, judgements and commentaries for Hexagram 1, *The Creative,* as well as for the top two lines of the hexagram. You would also look at the image, judgement and commentary for the second hexagram, Hexagram 34, *The Power of the Great.*

Every hexagram and every line within the hexagram has symbolic meaning. In a particular reading the hexagram as a whole, as well as any moving lines and second hexagram, contribute to your understanding of your question and your situation. The appended images, judgements and commentaries are to help clarify the appropriate attitudes and actions (or non-actions) necessary to stay in tune with the unfolding or flow of the Tao.

When a particular hexagram is cast (now often using computer programs, which seem to be no less effective than the traditional methods!) the *I Ching* gives guidance as to the best course of action to remain in harmony with the flow and rhythm of the Tao. The coins or stalks are cast in such a way that they fall at random into numerical patterns. Jung proposed that the random falling of the coins or stalks can be regarded as synchronous with the actual circumstances and events of the querent's life. The fall of the coins is in a relationship of synchronicity with the events in question. In the view of the *I Ching* the apparently random fall of coins or sticks is somehow expressive of an underlying pattern to the events of your life. Coins or sticks and life events all somehow express this pattern. The particular pattern of coins or stalks then refers to a particular reading in the *I Ching*. This reading, with its accompanying images, judgement and commentary, is thus in synchronous connection with the actual life situation and circumstances of the querent.

We may not be in touch with our own naturalness, our own pace and pulse, or our sense of our own place in the larger wholes of culture, nature and cosmos. Thus we often live by trying to force things or by imposing ideas of how things should be on ourselves, others and the world. When we see and feel the way things are, rather than the way we d like them to be, and allow ourselves to be guided, this is called following the Tao.

This process builds a physical bridge (the use of the coins or stalks) by which the "great one" or the "sage" (the one that speaks through the *I Ching*) can speak to the actual situation and circumstances of our physical life. An actual bridge with actual specific and practical results.[43]

This introduction to Chinese philosophy and the *I Ching* isn't meant to be at all comprehensive. For that, readers can go to the various editions of the *I Ching*, especially Richard Wilhelm's classic translation with a foreword by C.G. Jung. My purpose is more to find a way to approach the *I Ching* and especially the concepts of yin and yang from the perspective of oneness world, twoness world and intermediary world. Is there anything we can add to the classical understanding of these two principles, when seen through the lens of oneness, twoness and intermediary?

We have seen that yang is represented by an unbroken line and yin by a broken line. In Wilhelm's translation, we find the following: "Originally *chi* is the ridgepole – a simple line symbolising the positing of oneness (———). This positing of oneness implies also a positing of duality, an above and below. The conditioning element is further designated as an undivided line, while the conditioned element is represented by means of a divided line (—— ——). These are the two polar primary forces later designated as yang, the light principle, and yin, the dark."[44] So in this traditional image oneness is suggested (the ridgepole of the dwelling). And oneness gives rise to twoness (above and below) – that is, creates the conditions for twoness.

Thus the yang line represents something whole and unbroken. Let's say that it represents oneness. On the other hand the yin line could represent something divided. It could represent twoness.

This suggests an unbroken whole (oneness world) on the one hand, and on the other, the divided world of separate events and objects that we perceive – especially the separation of perceiver and perceived, of subject and object. So the *I Ching* posits two worlds or realities. One in which there is no separation, and one of (apparently) separate objects and events. Do you experience a single flow or a world of separation? What do you focus on, the separation or the wholeness? Do you experience oneness or twoness, or both?

Nigel Richmond, a little known *I Ching* researcher, writes of the trigram *Ch'ien* (in the *I Ching* a trigram is a unit of three lines; there are only eight possible combinations of yin and yang lines in units of three lines; *Ch'ien* is three unbroken yang lines – the trigram at the top of the figure below): "All the lines are whole. Reality is undivided, nothing is distinguished and so nothing is manifest. Distinguishing things requires a point of view and in the whole reality of *Ch'ien* there is no point of view chosen; it is the state of all points of view from which identities create the choice of their objects in time. So *Ch'ien* is 'the creative' or spiritual source; it is known as 'heaven' also." Richmond continues: "so Ch'ien in this elemental male role is the creator of relative reality; in this it is potentially active and is often known as 'the potential'. It is a celebration of wholeness."[45]

The eight trigrams

So yang could point to the background unbroken wholeness (oneness), also known as 'heaven', which although unbroken and whole is at the same time the creative source of all difference, of all that exists in spacetime in webs of cause-and-effect relationships (twoness). Likewise, in Bohm's map, the implicate order is whole and unbroken, but nevertheless holds the potential for anything that could exist in spacetime (the explicate order).

I'll return to a comparison with Bohm's proposals. But first there's another question. What about the Tao itself? Can we say anything about it and how might we conceive of it in relation to what's been said so far concerning oneness and twoness, and yang and yin.

In chapter 42 of the Taoist classic, the *Tao Te Ching*, Lao Tzu says:

The tao begot one.
One begot two.
Two begot three.
And three begot the ten thousand things.[46]

So something begets one which begets two. It's interesting to recall Bohm's model here – the holomovement, the implicate order and the explicate order. The holomovement is the unbroken whole beneath everything. We have already seen that "what 'carries' an implicate order is the *holomovement*, which is an unbroken and undivided totality… thus, *the holomovement is undefinable and immeasurable.*"

The implicate order is also whole and unbroken but contains all possibilities. So we might say it's the oneness world, symbolised by the unbroken yang line. Next, one begets two. Two gives birth to a third and thus the ten thousand things (symbolising the totality of all possible phenomena in spacetime). The explicate order arises.

So out of the Tao comes oneness (the unbroken yang line). And out of oneness comes twoness (the broken yin line). Twoness as a pair of opposites, the primal male and female, becomes a creative source without which the world of multiplicity would not exist. For things to exist, grow and evolve it is necessary for the two to give birth to a third, giving rise to the world of apparently separate objects and events in spacetime.

The Tao itself, although the origin of everything, is completely beyond definition or description – even beyond any notion of oneness or unity or undividedness. For the moment we posit the notion of undividedness, then there immediately arises the possibility of dividedness or twoness. The Tao is beyond all (but contains all) such possible definitions, polarities or contradictions.

Let's now try and look at all this more in terms of our own consciousness and experience. Let's say things might be something like this. Once upon a time, in the time before time, somehow, somewhere and at some time, out of the formless origin of all, the Tao, consciousness arose. This consciousness is the oneness that proceeds from the Tao. We could think of this consciousness as a point (maybe a point of light) in the endless darkness and emptiness of space. This consciousness is a kind of contraction of the nothing. In a certain sense this consciousness posits the existence of an 'I', a subject, something that is conscious, and in some sense conscious of itself. As soon as there is an 'I' – as soon as there is light in the ultimate darkness – the 'I' as consciousness seeks something to be conscious of. So one inevitably leads to two. There is unlimited emptiness, then there is a point of consciousness, with the potential for self-consciousness. This point of consciousness introduces a differentiation into emptiness. This original consciousness, being self-conscious, also has the capacity to become conscious of 'other', and eventually of 'an-other'. Once there is one and another the process of differentiation is initiated. There progressively comes into consciousness, and thus into being, the many others. The ten thousand things.

This is an understanding of oneness and twoness seen in terms of the emergence of consciousness. How does all this look in terms of our own beginnings and our own individual development? In human terms we start conscious, but without consciousness of things. Actually from the psychological perspective it would be said that we start as unconscious, because there is as yet little or no consciousness of 'I' as a separate entity, and thus little or no consciousness of the 'other'. Nevertheless, we can say that consciousness is present, even though it is as yet not conscious of itself or of things.

In the early months of our infant consciousness an awareness emerges of the difference between inner and outer. The infant starts to differentiate between sensations that have their origin within the body and those that originate from outside the body. The foundations of an awareness that I am different or separate from my environment are being established. My body is different from my physical surroundings. At some point in the developmental process there also arises the dawning awareness of another. There comes not just the awareness of the world giving rise to various sensations, but the awareness of other living creatures, especially humans, who have movements, actions and reactions that can arouse our happiness or unhappiness. There are others out there! Others that can make us happy or unhappy. This dawning of awareness of the other represents the birth of the emotional world, the emotional stage of development.

The earliest and most primal and encompassing presence of the other for the infant is the mother (m-other). For most human beings the presence or absence of the mother (or mother figure), with all the possibilities of satisfaction, frustration, safety and danger that implies, powerfully conditions our relationship with the world, especially our world of relationships. Patterns of attachment and dependency, and of wanting, rejecting or separating are created in the relationship with the primal other, your mother. Then in the course of time an outer world of objects and an inner world of likes and dislikes (desires and aversions) is born. As development proceeds, those outer objects and those inner likes and dislikes will become named – all those inner and outer things and events will become named objects. A world of multiplicity is born.[47]

Let's return to Lao Tzu:

The way that can be told
Is not the constant way:
The name that can be named
Is not the constant name.
The nameless was the beginning of heaven and earth;
The named was the mother of the myriad creatures.[48]

This passage indicates that the origin and sustainer of all is the nameless, formless Tao. A formlessness that sustains all forms. But there is also an emphasis on naming. There is nothing other than the unbroken whole. There is nothing other than wholeness, oneness. Humans, however, create an apparent world of separation through naming. This is what Lao Tzu's words suggest. At some point, or over a long period, in the distant past, humans learnt to name things, creating a world of multiplicity, so that they could manipulate the world and survive. This process, the origins of which lie far back in antiquity, is re-created in every human infant, in each one of us. We each build a picture of the world along with an inner world of desires and aversions, all of which we must recognise and name, in our attempt to survive, to be independent and secure.

Back to traditional Chinese philosophy. We can view the hexagrams of the *I Ching* as mappings of the interplay of the two primary principles of yin and yang playing out in natural phenomena. The two lines, the undivided and the divided, represent active and passive revealing themselves in fire and water, man and woman, valley and mountain, sun and moon, summer and winter and so on.

But might we also understand the hexagrams as mappings of the interplay of implicate and explicate? Of the interplay of the undivided and the divided in an unfolding orchestrated and held by the nameless, formless Tao and, in Bohm's understanding, the holomovement. (It's interesting that Tao is sometimes translated as "way", which also suggests motion). Could we see each hexagram as a mapping of oneness (implicate) unfolding in twoness (explicate, spacetime)?

Could there also be a parallel between the notion of oneness and twoness and the Chinese concept of yang and yin? As noted, the yang line is unbroken and the yin line is broken. We also note that the yang line represents potential, and is referred to as heaven, reminding us of Bohm's implicate order. Yin, the broken line, represents the world of duality, symbolised by the idea of earth. We recall the notion of twoness and Bohm's idea of the explicate order, where potential is realised in spacetime, in which apparently separate things and events are governed by the laws of physics.

This would put a slightly different slant on any question addressed to the *I Ching*. The question wouldn't only be, "where am I in the cycle of events?" "Where am I in the upward and downward curve of events?" "Is this particular situation in the ascendency or in decline?" "Am I in the springtime or summer or autumn of the cycle referred to (explicitly or implicitly) in my question?" All such cycles, events and patterns are governed by laws which we must do our best to understand and submit to. In the *I Ching's* philosophy, to do so is to support 'good fortune' and minimise 'misfortune'.

The question would also be what is trying to unfold from the creative source (oneness, implicate) into the spacetime conditions of earthly events (twoness, explicate)? What from beyond spacetime, and unconditioned by spacetime, could show up in spacetime?

The *I Ching* states that our life on earth is conditioned and unfree. We are conditioned by patterns in life, in nature, in our own nature and in the whole cosmos. The attempt to override this conditioning leads into difficulty. But what the *I Ching* also teaches (along with other spiritual traditions) is that we aren't just of the earth. We also belong to oneness. Our essential being is beyond spacetime and beyond the cycles of life and death. This doesn't mean that we are free to do what we want once we understand this. In fact, if anything, the reverse is true. The further we go and the more we deepen into ourselves, the more we realise how completely we are an expression of our patterns and our conditioning. So perhaps my creativity and possibly my freedom also lies in the fact that I can choose to try and harmonise with pre-ordained patterns, rather than try to impose my will, regardless. Perhaps our only real choice is to try to be aware, or not?

The *I Ching* is clear, again and again, about one thing. None of this is ultimately a matter of human will. Rather it is a matter of the recognition of, and capacity to harmonise with, what is. Timing is everything. To be in time and in tune. The sage surrenders to and follows the Tao. This is the art. This is the work.

When consulted, the *I Ching* responds (actually we can imagine the *I Ching* as a presence unlimited by spacetime, but present, conscious and engaged in spacetime) to practical questions that seek advice on how to proceed or act in a given situation or circumstance. In its answers it suggests ways of seeing things, and thus approaches to situations, which aren't based on habitual reactions. It seeks to shed light on underlying questions that can be present when you're faced with difficult choices or conflicted situations – "what is trying to happen?", "what direction should I take?", "how should I respond to this situation?", "what will be the outcome of such and such an action?". Those that created the *I Ching* sought a method which allows you to see your situation from a more expansive perspective. The method aims to give practical advice on how to act, when to act, when not to act, when to go forward, when to hold back and so on. It seeks to advise you on the practical business of staying in tune with the all-pervading now as it expresses itself in the river of time and the extension of space.

9. Oneness, Twoness and Creativity

The discussion of *the creative* in the last chapter brings us naturally to the question of our own human creativity. What is it? Where does it come from? Let's go back to Jung and synchronicity. According to Jung, synchronicity refers to events that are meaningfully connected despite the lack of any demonstrable causal connections. The appearance of such connected events might therefore be regarded, Jung says, as "creative acts."[49] Let's explore this a little more and think about creativity from the perspective of this inquiry into the oneness world and the twoness world.

Things that happen in the world of twoness are determined by the laws discovered by Newton and Einstein. Things (electrons, people, planets) are bound together in spacetime through cause and effect and action and reaction. In spacetime things have an effect on each other, via fields in which nothing travels faster than the speed of light. Effects are not instantaneous. Time is involved and thus creates a past and a future.

So why did Jung refer to synchronistic events as creative acts? Synchronistic events occur of course in the spacetime world but they don't originate in the twoness world. Rather they can be thought of as an expression of the oneness world in the twoness world. This overlap of oneness and twoness I've also termed the intermediary world, and the world of the intermediary.

The oneness world isn't defined by spacetime or by the laws governing the relationships and interactions of separate objects. It isn't defined by spacetime, by separation or by past and future.

From this perspective, events, as well as being connected through cause and effect according to the laws of spacetime, might also be acausally connected. That is to say that in the world of our experience both things can happen. Things can happen which are caused by something else – like the motion of a ball that's been kicked, or pain resulting from nerve stimulation, or the gravitational pull of the sun on the earth. Or things can happen which are meaningfully related but don't have any demonstrable cause-and-effect relationship – like precognition of yet-to-occur events, or receiving apparently meaningful or accurate guidance in response to a question put to an oracle such as the *I Ching*.

Events connected through cause and effect belong to the spacetime world. They are the content and activity of the twoness world – whether electrons, people, planets or galaxies. Then there's the other kind of event. Events that are connected, but not through spacetime laws. They are connected in our perception and our experience. But these connections nevertheless have an effect. They have an impact on us. Such connections can alter lives, tell us things we couldn't directly know, and even bring about healing in mind and body. Such connections suggest a background reality undefined by cause and effect and by spacetime.[50]

What kind of sense can we make of this? I have suggested that oneness so to speak 'pokes through' into twoness. In a certain sense oneness appears in twoness. When the oneness world appears in the twoness world such events are not defined by spacetime and cause and effect. They're coming out of a now which contains all possibilities and where something that happens isn't a reaction to something else. In the twoness world things happen as a reaction to something else. Actions are really more reactions. Things happen according to what went before. History is created. This is how it is in the twoness world.

What might all this mean in terms of our human experience and our human creativity? Let's try to make a distinction between reacting – born out of our conditioning and the conditions in which we find ourselves – and a 'creative act' unconditioned by the past. It's not that creativity is 'better' than reaction. But on a human level it's important to spot the difference between acting in a manner which is less conditioned by our past, and re-acting, which is more conditioned by our experience.

One definition of creativity is, therefore, that it brings something new. It's not a reaction. Not something defined by what went before (in spacetime or in history). So we could say that whenever we find ourselves creating or doing or thinking something that has an element of surprise to it – we hadn't worked out previously how to do it, or we don't know how we got to this time and place where we seem to be creating, doing or thinking something which seems new, unusual, surprising – we're somehow connected with the oneness world, the unity beyond spacetime and the laws of action and reaction, and are thus participating in a creative act.

We could be talking here about something like a piece of art, music or dance. Or we could be talking about daily life activity – making tea, cooking, cleaning. Either way there's the possibility of a kind of timelessness, or a newness or freshness. There might be a sense of something just happening without any special intention or effort on our part. (Of course if it's a creative project there might have been intention and effort. Lots of it. Isn't it said that genius is 10% inspiration and 90% perspiration? We might say that the 10% belongs to the oneness world and the 90% belongs to the twoness world!) At such times we might experience a sense of timelessness, or that a short time seems much longer. We've probably all had moments such as these. Sports people speak of this timeless effortless place as "being in the zone."

The point is that such times aren't especially linked to what went before. For example, improvising musicians or dancers might have the sense of creating something in movement or sound, that although coming after what went before or what just happened, and in that sense built on what went before, is nevertheless not conditioned by what went before. It doesn't copy what went before or react to what went before. It might include what went before (sequences of movement, musical riffs) but somehow brings something new which can't entirely be predicted or explained by what went before. In terms of my model of oneness and twoness, this is oneness appearing in twoness. Actually in these moments the dancer or the musician might have the sense of something just happening, of creation just happening by itself, without a doer or a sense that 'I' am doing it.

Another distinction which might be helpful here is that between reactivity and responsiveness. Reaction, as we've seen, is born out of twoness. Response, in the sense suggested here, is more like an opening to what is needed in a given situation. It doesn't react to. Rather it gives to. In this sense it has the hallmark of oneness. Of course, to be responsive to a situation might mean being freer from one's own conditioning and one's own notions of what is right or wrong in a given situation. If you're developing the capacity to be responsive, in the way suggested here, it may mean you're doing significant work on yourself – work that involves not only more self-awareness, but emptying and letting go as well. We need to allow more empty space, freer of our own ideas about how things are. This can also mean, over time, giving up elements of our identity and beliefs, especially those that shore up our sense of a fixed self, a definite 'somebody'. For most of us, doing this goes against the grain. We'd far rather stay in what we know, than be born into the unknown. We'd far rather be full of a sense of self than to be an empty vessel. But how can the unknown arrive if there's no empty cup to receive it?

It might seem, in this short inquiry into reactivity and responsiveness, that there's a stark choice. Either I'm reactive or I'm responsive. Or, either I'm creative or I'm reacting out of habit. It's not my intention to make such an unyielding contrast. After all, without a highly tuned capacity to react how long would our ancestors have survived?

Perhaps it's more helpful to think in terms of a kind of dance, between our sense of self and something more open and expansive. Or, put another way, between the personal and the transpersonal. It's not a question of getting rid of the 'me'. But we could think of the me as a kind of container. And of allowing the container to be more expansive, more flexible, so that which is beyond the me, and not defined by the me, can somehow appear in the me, inform the me. The 'other-than-me' can begin to shape and inform the me. Oneness can shape and inform twoness.

It might also seem, from what I've said here, that creativity and connection to oneness is somehow special and unusual. It might seem that we need to go beyond our normal self to achieve it. It might seem that such connection is super-natural and not natural.

But it might be that such connection, such openness, is available and here far more than we think. Such connection and harmony with the timeless oneness world could be natural rather than super-natural. Maybe when we're in the flow, attending to what's happening, rather than trying to make things happen, oneness is right here in twoness as a natural part of life. The result – things work out. The right person shows up at the right time. We're in the right place at the right time. Even when things have seemed difficult or delayed. But we have to be attentive. Notice all our sensations and feelings. Notice what's happening around us. Not driven by reactive needs and desires. Not in a state of knowing, but of unknowing. Then the creativity, the freshness might be here moment to moment.

In this chapter I've approached the question of creativity and in the next chapter we'll consider healing and wholeness in a similar light.

10. Oneness, Twoness and Healing

I've suggested that creativity can be thought of as coming out of a nowness free of past conditioning. In this sense creativity emerges from beyond the definition, conditioning and history characteristic of the twoness world, into the conditions of spacetime.

Can we approach the question of healing from a similar point of view? By the term healing I don't mean only the correction of dysfunctional parts, such as dysfunctional organs and systems of the body. Rather I mean the business of making whole. One can intervene with surgery to help a damaged organ, or one can give a drug with a specific action on an organ, system or symptom. Doing this may constitute medical practice, but doesn't necessarily constitute making whole – healing the whole person.

Healing, in the sense used here, means helping to free the capacity to think, feel and act from more or less conditioned habit. To be healed, or to be in the process of being healed, means being less reactive – less conditioned by one's reactions. It could mean there's more space. There's less tendency to be fixed in our thinking (obsessive tendency), and less tendency to be fixed in our behaviour (compulsive tendency). It means less reliance on a fixed image or fixed sense of self. One is less embedded in the twoness world with its dynamics of action and reaction. There's more flexibility, more flow. (Although it's beyond the scope of this book, it's possible to demonstrate that such changes as these, occurring during a healing process, can be accompanied by curative changes in dysfunctional systems and organs of the body. In other words I'm here describing a capacity for healing that can take place in the whole mind/body/energy system. Such healing isn't just confined to positive alterations in emotional well-being or psychological outlook.)

We can say, in general, that newborns and infants are more open and unstructured. Therefore there's less defence against what comes in. All sensory impressions, whether pleasurable, painful or harmful, flow in. The unprotected little one can only receive and react. As long as natural reactions to pleasure or pain (laughing, crying, flinching, starting, etc.) aren't repressed, the developing nervous system has the possibility of remaining relatively balanced and healthy. (Of course, physical reactions such as fever or skin conditions, which might also be reactions to all manner of physical or psychological stress, are also vitally important, and should not be unnecessarily suppressed.)[51]

But when during the course of development, reactions to hurt, trauma or other harmful influences – reactions that were once healthy, normal and necessary – become fixed into patterns of reaction, or into feelings of absence and lack, the flow and spontaneity of life becomes hampered. This is, from the perspective taken here, the beginning of dysfunction and disease. Our way of being becomes more limited and fixed and less adaptable and flexible. We then carry the burden of old habits and reactions. Our inner life becomes an expression of polarity more than flow. The world of conflict and opposition can become our reality. This duality informs our way of being, our way of cognition, and eventually it shows up in our bodies as dysfunction and disease.

It seems then, that in the course of our individual development, natural openness, sensitivity and reactiveness can be reduced, while a more fixed and patterned way of being and reacting can be strengthened. We then learn to believe that this is who we are. My conditioned reactions with their accompanying thoughts and beliefs become part of my sense of who I am. It's not really who I am, but I may become more identified with these patterns and come to believe that's who I am.

Behind this there is still intrinsic openness and unstructured flow. There is still capacity for being, for flow, for sensitivity. There is still the capacity for appropriate reaction to environment, to circumstances, to others. And critically there is still the capacity for appropriate reaction to harmful, hurtful or traumatic influences.

But almost inevitably, at some point in our development, things close down. Sensitivity is reduced or protected. Patterns of reactivity and defence are established. Defences and reactions can become exaggerated. Of course, these patterns can take myriad forms. They can also have different levels of severity. If you've been well loved and supported, your reactions aren't going to be as fixed or as serious as they are if you've not been loved, or you've been mistreated or abused. But the tendency to form reactive patterns is there in all of us to one degree or another. And in some people these reactive patterns can become very fixed, very habitual, and sometimes damaging to self and others.

If we suffered in life, defensive patterns came into being for good reason, possibly to protect us from a harsh or abusive environment. But these patterns also become quite mixed up in who we feel we are, in our sense of ourselves. They become inextricably wound up with our sense of self, with our identity. From the perspective taken here we can say that healing involves a moving from overly structured patterning and identity to the openness, sensitivity and flow of our essential nature.

How does all this look in the context of oneness world and twoness world? Healing, or making whole, can follow when more openness comes into our structure. Then the structure that I call 'me' can itself become more flexible. The emphasis is on the openness and responsiveness of oneness, rather than the fixed reactions of twoness. In this sense healing calls on oneness.

Let me try and put this another way. In the perspective I've taken here, disease and duality are bedfellows. In the course of our development separation occurs. First we get separated from our mother. Then, as we develop, parts of ourselves get shut down, pushed out, denied. We could say that outer separation gives birth to inner separation. In the service of survival it's only natural that we learnt to favour some of our characteristics, feelings and actions, and to repress others. Original wholeness and cohesiveness gives way to dis-integration. We become beings of many parts, some in the light, others not. Separation is at the root of our experience of ourselves. And it might also be that this separation, painful and dysfunctional as it can be, eventually prompts us to take the journey of self-discovery, from dis-integration to re-integration.

If being born and subsequent suffering rests on the bed of separation, of duality, of twoness, then twoness cannot also give rise to healing and wholeness. But there is at the same time a paradox here. To find wholeness we must look deeply into our brokenness, our duality, our separation.

In a sense the container must break. The seed pod or pupa that protects us, also keeps us separate. We have to outgrow what once protected us. We're surrounded by oneness, but our sense of self and the need to be 'somebody' can be an obstacle. Also, paradoxically, unless you become a person, unless you individuate (Jung's term suggesting living into your individuality as fully as possible), with some inevitable separation and suffering, how can you transcend your personhood and become the space where the personal and the transpersonal become one?

From this point of view, healing, like creativity, begins to look like a procedure or practice whereby oneness can enter and make its presence known in twoness.

11. Dreams, Science and the Intermediary World

I want now to touch on a subject and area of experience that almost everybody can relate to – dreams.

Dreams have always fascinated us. They turn up right here in our twoness world experience but we sense they come from somewhere else. They often picture twoness world events and conflicts, yet they mainly occur at night, during sleep, when the twoness world is shut out. They often seem to refer to everyday events but at the same time can seem strange and unknowable. And people have always asked "what do they mean?"

We have known for over a hundred years now about the subconscious and the regulatory function of dreams.[52] They redress the balance in the psyche, helping to keep equilibrium between the conscious and unconscious parts of ourselves. They may also function as something akin to a digestive process, digesting everyday experience. These aspects of dreams, the balancing function and the digestive function, seem largely to belong to the twoness world of cause and effect and action and reaction.

That dreams can also be clairvoyant or precognitive is well noted throughout history. Dreams of this nature may be a common experience, but easily dismissed in our scientific age. Rupert Sheldrake has suggested (based on data collected by him) that dreams can be precognitive more frequently than we think.[53] (In a psychological age people tend to look for meaning in their dreams and can overlook the precognitive aspect.) He notes that people often dream of events about to happen, and refers to J.W. Dunne's classic work, *An Experiment with Time*, in which Dunne reports that, through keeping a careful record of his own dreams, he found that he often dreamed of events yet to happen. Dunne makes a serious attempt to develop a model of time in which the future as well as the past is accessible to consciousness.

So it seems that dreams can, sometimes at least, be unconfined by spacetime. The dreams reported by Dunne and other researchers – dreams that show glimpses of events yet to occur – are not necessarily especially significant for the dreamer. But they are enough to demonstrate the capacity of the subconscious mind to reach beyond our natural time-frame, a time-frame in which we have access to events of the past, but not to events that haven't yet occurred.

Such mapping of the future may be literal. For example, you might dream of someone unknown to you, and subsequently unexpectedly meet or hear from that person. There's lots of anecdotal evidence for such precognitive dreams. Dreams of the future might of course be as inexplicable as other dreams, and might even have no personal relevance for the dreamer.

Nevertheless dreams often picture something unknown to us, but which we need to know for our health, our development, our balance, our integrity, and sometimes for our or someone else's survival. Such dreams could say something about the present, the past, or the future. Sometimes it seems that the dreaming self can have a perspective not limited by our normal experience of sequential time.

I remember an occasion when I was the person dreamt of by someone who had never met me. This man came as a guest to a class I was giving on dreams. At the end he asked: "What does it mean when you dream of someone you don't know, and then you meet that person?" I didn't know what to say, and probably didn't give a very satisfactory answer. Anyway I then said "who was the person you dreamt of?" His answer came, "you". I was taken aback. Why should he have dreamt of me before we had ever met? Of course he might have heard about me, or even seen a picture of me. Even if that were so, what followed was still strange and unusual. When we met there was as yet no answer to this question. But a kind of answer soon became clear. At the time of our meeting I had recently experienced a tragic death in my immediate family. Looking back I can say I was walking in the shadow of death. At the time neither I nor this man, the dreamer, could know that he too would shortly be dead, again through an unexpected tragic accident.

The capacity for such dreaming has probably been observed and reported since time immemorial. For the modern scientist all such reports are anecdotal and prove nothing. However, there is a growing body of modern research that supports such anecdotal data. Sheldrake offers a number of examples of premonition (warning in advance), precognition (knowing in advance), and presentiment (feeling in advance). He has also created simple experiments to show that such things are possible, whether occurring in dreams or when awake.[54] He has also suggested that such capacities may be considered natural rather than supernatural. It's often reported, for example, that animals have sensed the approach of natural disasters long before humans are aware that there's anything wrong. Such abilities, whether found in animals or humans, could have survival value.

Science and scientists mostly dismiss events such as precognitive dreams or meaningful synchronicities as impossible, unreal or imagined. Why?

Despite the contradictions and apparent impossibilities revealed in quantum mechanics, the current scientific model will generally only accept a reality where cause and effect can clearly be demonstrated, and where the observer or the experimenter is excluded from any model of reality. Science wants to establish what is objectively true. And of course this is right. This is where human knowledge needs to evolve. As a species we need to be able to establish what is true, independent of the subjective states of observers and experimenters (see final chapter).

But when approaching the intermediary world – the world of synchronicity, of inexplicable connections, the world of the shaman, the world where established laws of spacetime might not hold up, we run into problems. (Actually it's not just in such phenomena as synchronicity that this might be so. Quantum mechanics has also revealed such a world right at the heart of the modern scientific model of reality).

The intermediary world is the world of inexplicable occurrences and connections. It is the world of precognition and clairvoyance. The world of oracles. The world of healing methodologies science can find no explanation for. It is also a kind of bridge to creativity (see chapter 9). It is therefore also, in a certain sense, the world of the imagination. This means that the artist or scientist can sometimes open to a kind of creativity undictated by spacetime – to something coming from the future, from the realm of the not-yet-happened. But, of course, this very same imagination can be the source of both creativity and of delusion and error.

Thus for the scientific mind the intermediary world and everything that belongs to it must be dismissed. It isn't measurable and doesn't obey known scientific laws. It's also the world in which our inner experience can somehow be entangled with outer events. And scientists aren't the first to dismiss the reality of this intermediary world. It was dismissed and outlawed by the Christian Church as the source of delusion and madness, and the home of powers and demons that would lead us astray. Any hint of it must be ruthlessly suppressed.

When we come to the world of precognition and of synchronicity, here's the problem. Science wants, rightly, to establish what's objectively true. What's true for all humans? What can all humans agree on, because it's shown, regardless of subjective opinion, to be true? But the world of inexplicable events and connections isn't only objective. It's subjective as well. Objective events are somehow related to subjective conditions. The hard boundary between objective fact and subjective perception turns out to be not so hard and fast after all. It's more porous than that.

Jung has proposed that synchronicity, precognition and other related phenomena, where events are connected across space and time in the absence of any apparent cause-and-effect mechanism, don't simply arise on neutral ground. They depend on conditions of readiness, urgency, expectation, and psychic charge in the individuals or groups involved. Then inner and outer can be intertwined in a pattern that's somehow unrestricted by spacetime laws of cause and effect. A pattern that can be playing out inwardly and outwardly and revealing itself in more than one location simultaneously, as for example in the simultaneous inner state of a querent using the *I Ching* oracle, and the apparently random fall (outward activity) of the coins or yarrow stalks. Jung proposed that such patterns are archetypes – fundamental patterns at the root of our thinking and our instinctual life.

As we'll see in the final chapter, modern science, having established the very necessary protocols for objectivity, doesn't know what to do with subjectivity. Despite the quantum mechanical description of reality, scientists in general still cannot find a place for subjectivity in the observation of nature and in empirical protocols. But all the phenomena discussed here – synchronicity, oracle readings, dreams – represent a kind of meeting of our inner state with objective reality.

Returning to dreams and our relationship with them, another problem is that they can be partly or wholly symbolic. A symbol, according to Jung, points to something unknown and possibly unknowable.[55] It goes beyond words. Words dissect and take apart and thus represent a limited point of view. A symbol is intrinsically whole. Think of dreaming of a cup, or holding a cup, as opposed to reading a description of a cup. The dreams that have had the greatest impact on me have been symbolic.

It's possible that symbols show up in our dreams via the intermediary world. And they may come to us from our own future, from a future outside our normal time-frame. These kinds of dreams might not be so much about where we've been as where we're going. They're attractors attracting us to our own future. As Sheldrake says in his discussion of attractors: "Developing systems are attracted towards their ends or goals. They are not only pushed from the past, they are pulled from the future." And: "some interpretations of quantum mechanics allow for physical influences working backwards in time or, in other words, causal influences from the future."[56]

So some dreams may have access to the future, tuning into events yet to occur, in a functional or pragmatic manner. Others may be altogether more mysterious, connecting to the future through symbols that function as attractors. Whether such dreams are literal or symbolic, it suggests a kind of cognition unconfined by spacetime and the laws of cause and effect.

Here's a dream of mine that was and is symbolic and significant for me, even though it occurred around thirty years ago.

Although such a dream will appear in a specific time and place, perhaps in response to a current situation, what it alludes to often seems to go far beyond our current situation. Once again it seems that it's our needs in this time and place that call forth a specific response from something other, in much the same way that, according to Jung, psychic conditions call forth synchronistic events. Such a dream, although coming at a certain time and place, is, I suggest, not spacetime specific and could unfold its meaning over years or decades.

In the dream I'm around the age of 13 going downhill on the red and white racing bike I had at that age. I'm going fast, freewheeling. It's a tarmac road, and about half way down a railway track crosses the road. And as is often the case, the track as it crosses the road is embedded in the road, forming double grooves going across the road. Going at speed I wobble as I cross the tracks and nearly lose control, but I'm ok. I don't fall off, and keep on going downwards. I eventually get to the bottom of the road, which is also the bottom of the valley. There's a tree growing there, and I get off my bike and go and lean it against the tree. I notice that there's something like a crystal pineapple growing in the tree. I reach up and pluck it.

This dream is as fresh today as it was when I had it. For me it still looks and feels significant. From the perspective of depth psychology it has archetypal characteristics. The downward journey. The tree. The crystalline fruit.

In my understanding the dream pictures a downward journey. I'll call it a soul journey to the depth, rather than a spiritual journey to the height. I come from the height and am carried downwards. In this downward trajectory there's a real danger of instability – of being badly derailed. In my own life I've had plenty of opportunity to experience exactly what this might mean. It's also a journey towards something special and precious. The idea of a many-faceted crystal like the crystal pineapple in the dream is similar to something found in many spiritual traditions. The diamond body for instance. It symbolises the essence of who we are. Materialised light as it were. Jung would see in such an image a symbol of the self, our true essence that is unfolding in this life.

The symbolism of this dream is important. But what I want to emphasise here is the pathway by which something from beyond spacetime – something non-spacetime specific – appears in a spacetime specific form. The dream occurred in a specific time and place. But its content, in my understanding, isn't spacetime specific. The dream seems to me to embody a story, or we could say soul trajectory, that is unfolding through time. The wisdom contained within the dream could be said to come from a domain unfettered by space and time. This could explain why the dream is still so significant today, and why its message is still deepening, still coming home to me.

I was told once by the Dzogchen teacher Namkhai Norbu, having related my dream to him, that it was significant that I reached up to pluck the crystalline fruit. The dream may say something about the difficulties of my path in life – assuming of course that I have the ears to hear. But it may also be an attractor. That is to say something that is at once personal to me, but nevertheless unlimited by spacetime, something 'other'. An attractor comes from a future that in some sense already exists. But this future must be outside the cause-and-effect world described by science (twoness world). Perhaps the act of reaching up to pluck this object was itself a creative act coming from the oneness world? That is to say, an act coming out of the spaciousness and spontaneity of the moment, rather than an act as a reaction to something that went before – the difference between a free, unconditioned act, and an act as a conditioned response.

It may be that such dreams actually *come to us* from oneness. In such a dream the oneness world appears in our twoness world. In a certain time and place a need for change or for guidance arises in our individuality. There is some kind of openness or availability. Into this openness comes the creative expression of something beyond spacetime and beyond our personal self. In my example this takes the form of the dream. In this case the dream event is an expression of both the individual need and the creative response of that which is beyond spacetime and beyond individual self.

Let's return to the theme of oneness and twoness. But now taking a more expanded view through the lens of cultural and spiritual traditions and from a perspective that embraces the great archetypal symbols handed down to us from the past.

12. Oneness World and Twoness World: this world and that world

The world's spiritual traditions have sought to understand our human spacetime existence and our relationship to the oneness world. It's as though human beings always understood that this world of appearances is not our real home. Some spiritual traditions emphasise the fact that as a species and as individuals we forgot something. We forgot our true nature and our innate wholeness. In the Christian mystical tradition this is thought of as a fall from grace, a falling out of wholeness – an image that perhaps mirrors the downward motion of our physical birth. In the Buddhist tradition there's the idea of ignorance – that through birth we forgot our origins and true nature.

Both of these traditions point to a kind of unconsciousness. Whether thought of as an original fall or the onset of a state of ignorance, this unconsciousness is said, in the Buddhist tradition at least, to be at the root of suffering because it means we're deluded about our own true nature. And this forgetting, this delusion leads to endless error, trouble and suffering. So some spiritual paths require us to reset our perception. And this involves confronting the habitual ways of perceiving and acting that are built on the foundations of the primary delusion, the primary error.

Concerning the roots of human unconsciousness or suffering, the Christian and Buddhist approaches are a little different. Each highlights a somewhat different relationship to our original nature – the nature unconditioned by spacetime. To put it slightly differently, each highlights a different relationship to the oneness world, the reality that transcends spacetime. Here I won't emphasise these differences as religious differences, rather as different understandings inherent in the human soul. The fact that these different insights became enshrined in different religions needn't concern us here. What concerns us is the understanding of the oneness world and the twoness world that's inherent in cultural and religious traditions.

The Hindu tradition and the Buddhist tradition that grew out of it have, it seems to me, emphasised the oneness world. By this I mean the oneness world understood as the empty, formless reality that exists behind the world of form (twoness world).

The teaching of the formless oneness inherent in everything reaches perhaps its maturest expression in Advaita Vedanta in the Hindu tradition and Dzogchen in the Buddhist tradition. The insights expressed in these teachings can be summarised as follows. They state that our true nature is none other than, is identical with, the formless emptiness behind existence. It's not that you exist *in* the oneness world. To see it like that wouldn't make sense at all. If that were the case it would mean that there was a twoness in the oneness world. It would imply a subject (you) that experiences an object (reality). And, as we've seen, this can't be so in the oneness world. It only appears so in the twoness world.

The great teachers in these traditions tell us, from their own insight and experience that our true nature doesn't belong to the twoness world. We only have a temporary home in spacetime. Our true nature is eternal. In other words, it's part of the oneness world, unlimited and undefined by spacetime. They then make the most radical statement, draw the most radical conclusion possible. It's this. Since your real nature partakes of the oneness world, and there is no separation in the oneness world, no spacetime and no cause and effect, then each of us cannot be something other than the oneness world. Because, they say, in reality there isn't any this and that, there isn't any subject and object, there isn't any 'I' and 'other'.

They also maintain that this fact is as close to you as your own nose. It is simply there waiting to be discovered. But often we don't find it because we look everywhere else for something that is right here. This means we continue to experience ourselves as separate, and continue to experience a world of duality. We continue to take the twoness world as the fundamental reality. This, the traditions say, is ignorance, an error of perception.

The insight and understanding that arose in the Christian tradition is, it seems to me, rather different. If we approach the story of Christ as a symbolic understanding of our own true nature's relationship to the world, then the Christian spiritual tradition has emphasised the way in which the oneness world *comes into* the twoness world. Here we are led to understand, in a slightly different way than is presented in Advaita Vedanta, the relationship between oneness and twoness.

It seems to me that we're led to understand that oneness unfolds in – is born into – twoness. That which is beyond spacetime is born, as the divine being, into spacetime. This is what the Christian story, treated as a symbol, suggests. Oneness unfolds in twoness, gradually permeating twoness. Of course I'm speaking here as though this process is somehow happening 'out there'. It would be more accurate to say that this unfolding is really happening in consciousness itself. There is realisation of oneness.

I'll try and express this another way. The emphasis in Christian teaching and iconography is on love and on the heart. So we might say that the emphasis in the Christian tradition has been on our human longing for oneness, and at the same time – if one can really say this – the potential or longing of oneness to come into twoness. It seems to me that the emphasis in the Buddha's teaching and in Buddhism is knowledge of your true nature. The Buddhist is guided through the understanding of the reality of suffering, and through practice, to an experience of original nature. In the Christian tradition the emphasis is rather different. There is an emphasis on the longing of the heart. A longing for redemption, for forgiveness, for release. And this longing is answered by total love and acceptance. It is as though the longing goes both ways. In the language of oneness and twoness, twoness longs for oneness, and oneness longs to come into twoness.

This approach to, and understanding of, the oneness world and the twoness world would help to make sense of the image of Christ on the cross, not as a religious symbol, but as an archetypal symbol expressing something fundamental in the human condition. We could view this image as pointing to the "entry" of the oneness world into the twoness world. An aspect of oneness, symbolised by Christ, is shown suffering in the spacetime world of opposites (twoness), symbolised by the cross.

Perhaps also this is what the author of St. John's gospel was pointing to when they wrote "and the Word was made flesh."[57] This image suggests the entry of the creative aspect of the oneness world (*word*) into the twoness world of spacetime (*flesh*).

At this point we can also approach another image central to the story of Christ, the 'virgin birth'. When we approach this mystery as a symbol, what could it possibly mean? Normally a birth is the result of the coming together of male and female. This means that although we can say that something in the human being, the soul, comes from the oneness world, it is nevertheless born into the conditions of, and is conditioned by, the twoness world.

However we're told that the Christ child didn't take this route into the world. He was born of a virgin. What might this mean symbolically? Seen from this perspective a 'normal' birth, through the coming together of the opposites of male and female, suggests a new being coming into and being conditioned by the twoness world of spacetime, cause and effect and so on. But this doesn't happen in the Christ story. There is no coming together of the opposites. It's as though in the story of Christ's birth we have an image of oneness coming into the twoness world, but retaining its oneness. Oneness is born into the twoness world but isn't conditioned by twoness, isn't conditioned by spacetime and its history.

Vesica Piscis

The Vesica Piscis is formed of two equal circles with the centre of one lying on the circumference of the other. This geometrical form, along with the mathematical ratios contained within it, was important in the forms of sacred art and architecture of the past. (One of the ratios that can be obtained from the vesica piscis is the golden mean mathematical ratio – found in sacred art and architecture, as well as natural growth forms in plants).

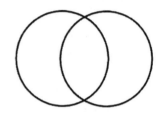

In one interpretation of this symbol we could imagine one circle representing the oneness world, the other circle the twoness world, and the vesica as the intermediary world (the realm of the intermediaries and of intermediary activity).

In Christian iconography Christ is often depicted in the central segment. The symbol suggests that our true essence, symbolised here by Christ, is of both the eternal (oneness world) and the temporal (twoness world). Christ (symbolising our essential self) can be understood as an intermediary, or as eternal presence born into twoness.

In a further interpretation we could imagine the vesica (central section) as the implicate order (in Bohm's map) which contains all possibilities within it. The implicate order stands between the pure empty potential of the oneness world (the holomovement in Bohm's map) and the realisation of separate stable forms in the twoness world (the explicate order in Bohm's map).

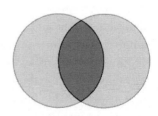

Let's try to follow these clues a little further into the Christian story. The Buddha taught human beings about their true nature. He showed human beings how they could know who they truly are – the eternal formlessness behind all form – ultimately beyond any notion of an individual self. The Christian story brings a new dimension to this understanding. The Christ story demonstrates the entry of oneness into twoness, symbolised as a birth. The story points to a reality in which oneness unfolds in twoness. It also shows oneness completely accepting and taking on the conditions of twoness, without itself becoming conditioned by twoness and losing its essential oneness, its nowness, free of history.

Of course, in the original story it's told that this birth takes place once at a particular time and place in spacetime. And in the Christian world this event is celebrated once a year. It's important for many people to have this historically related event to celebrate. But we can also think about this story in a way that liberates it from its specific cultural and religious setting. We can understand it regardless of religious and cultural considerations as fundamental presence that is wanting to unfold in the world.

So we can say that this birth is not a once only event. Rather it is a constant birthing which we can think of as the unfolding now, or the unfolding of eternal presence. It is as though there exists the possibility of a constant unfolding of oneness into twoness. What is beyond spacetime is constantly unfolding into spacetime. This unfolding happens in time, but doesn't originate in time. Timelessness unfolds in spacetime.

But we should not lose sight of the fact that the story does describe an event that took place at a specific time and place. From the perspective taken here, the fact that these events are described as happening in a specific time and place, and in a specific historical context, underlines that what's being spoken of is an appearance of the oneness world in twoness in a specific and definite manner. There's nothing airy-fairy here. Something's being referred to here that's real. It's real in the world. It's real flesh and blood. It's fully embodied. Fully here. The story doesn't refer to before time. It's very definitely *in* time.

I believe this unfolding is what the physicist David Bohm was also driving at, from the perspective of the completely different discipline of physics. The implicate order is the unbroken and complete ocean of potential which enfolds all possibilities. In this order everything is enfolded in everything else. There is no separation. But at the same time all possible differences exist in potential. This aspect of the oneness world is unbroken and whole, but all possible parts are there too, in potential. This is the paradox. These possibilities, these potentialities, are realised in the explicate order. In the explicate order possibilities are realised as apparently separate and stable forms, such as electrons, atoms, mineral elements, living organisms and so on.

The implications of the teachings that are presented in Christian theology are far-reaching indeed. In the East the emphasis has been on the return to oneness through self-knowledge and the loosening of the bonds of attachment. In the tradition that emerged in the Middle East and later the West the emphasis has been on seeing the spacetime world as becoming permeated by the oneness world. Another helpful image here could be that of darkness being suffused by light – the light of the rising sun permeating darkness.

We might now even make some sense of the notion of 'redemption of matter' found in Christian and alchemic mystical traditions.[58] This of course doesn't imply that matter is evil or bad. In fact it isn't matter at all that needs to be redeemed. It would make more sense to say that it's human consciousness that's in need of redemption. Human consciousness is limited by its perception of the twoness world, is identified with the material world and is thus in a state of conflict and separation. Nevertheless (putting it in the language of the past) we can say there is a process of redemption. Something of the eternal is unfolding in the extension of space and the river of time. In this revelation human consciousness is liberated from its identification with – a kind of imprisonment within – the world of things.

Of course, it would be a very limited view to focus only on human suffering. Animals suffer horribly, much of it perpetrated by humans. But do all creatures, and indeed all things, as well as humans, suffer a kind of feeling of, or a kind of awareness of, separation? Are all creatures – animals, plants, and even rocks, crystals and electrons – longing to belong, longing to go home? And is that longing an expression of joy or suffering? Does the notion of redemption of matter somehow hint at these unanswerable questions? Questions that probably can't even make sense to our rational minds.

But a word of caution here. The notion of redemption easily leads to the notion of sin, and then to the idea of denying or transcending our body. We are now well informed as to the consequences of such a cultural attempt to transcend or deny our bodies, instinct and earthly need. And much has also been written about the possibly inevitable consequences of the development of human self-consciousness. How consciousness, in its attempt to emancipate itself from its unconscious past, also turned on its own dear roots of instinct, warmth and sensory openness.[59]

But how to mend this tear in the human soul? How to give appropriate and proportional value to spirit and body, to above and below? It seems to me we're led, in the perspective set out above, to the need to embrace and experience our physical humanness. Perhaps this is what is meant by redemption? Nothing can be redeemed by denying it, by pushing it away. In this perspective, the more we can feel and experience ourselves, right down into our deeper feelings and sensations, the more chance there is of real healing. Allowing everything to be there as it is – our pain, our joy, our sensations, our feelings, our thoughts really opening ourselves to all of it, is already a tremendous act of commitment. And this approach also means that we're especially mindful about acting out. We're cautious about acting on our impulses, on our reactions, or our thoughts. Actually most of the time it means not acting. Non-action in the sense of not forcing things, not pushing, not imposing. As it says in the *Tao Te Ching*, the sage does nothing and yet nothing remains undone.

Of course, we do what needs to be done. But we don't do from a place of trying to get somewhere. Rather our attention is given to our experience, our feelings and sensations. We sit in any discomfort or pain we find there. We hold it in the sealed vessel of ourselves, our awareness, just as the alchemists hinted at through the symbols of their practice. Neither acting out nor suppressing. This is the work of gradual transformation which is, as far as I understand it, the path of healing.

On the one hand, in the Eastern tradition we're led to understand the eternal reality behind everything. And on the other, in the Middle Eastern and Western tradition, we're shown that there's a process unfolding in spacetime in which the oneness world takes on the mantle of the twoness world. This process is understood, in the Christian tradition anyway, as suffering that has to be accepted. After all, the story of Christ teaches us acceptance of the conditions of the twoness world without any kind of resistance. Of course, the teaching of love and compassion for all that suffers is central to both Buddhism and Christianity. But it seems to me that the Christian story – probably building on much older stories, such as that of Prometheus, who got chained to a rock for the sin of stealing fire from the gods – makes special allusion to our bodily reality and to our suffering the conditions (and conditioning) of spacetime, and possibly to a debt that has to be paid for the acquisition of self-consciousness.

Paradoxically this total acceptance of the conflicts and polarities of the twoness world is seen as the way to liberation. We don't find freedom through any kind of avoidance or transcendence of pain or conflict. That's not how it is at all. Jung once said that we have to drink our experience down to the very dregs. For me this means feeling and sensing our experience right to the core.

According to the Dzogchen teacher Namkhai Norbu, everything is striving for liberation.[60] For me this means that not only is everything 'out there' in the world wishing to be free to live as itself, but everything in us as well. This doesn't mean acting out our impulses and fantasies. But it does mean feeling and sensing all that goes on in our inner field of awareness – especially anything that's on the edge, trying to come into the light of our awareness. To have greater capacity in our sensing of ourselves, sensing what goes on often below the threshold of consciousness – in short to be more sensitive – we often need to step back more to allow space for what wants to be present, wants to be known. Everything wants to be seen, accepted, known, loved. Anything inside you, once completely felt, completely experienced, becomes 'known'. This is really all that's needed for 'spontaneous liberation'.

Beyond this there is really nothing to be done. Often our tendency when faced with pain, conflict or fear is to take the wrong kind of action. Action to remove, get rid of, remove from sight, from sense. But things, be they situations or symptoms, are never really solved like this. How can we solve something not known, not understood? The view expressed here involves a turning towards, an acceptance, a knowing – rather than a turning away from or opposition. As Norbu says, everything seeks spontaneous liberation. If something in us needs to become more conscious, all that is required is that we experience that feeling, or that sensation, as completely and as wholly without resistance as possible. Then that part can spontaneously liberate. That is to say it goes back into the light, like a child's soap bubble popping on a summer day. Or, in modern psychological parlance, it becomes integrated into our wholeness.

In one sense it doesn't matter whether we're speaking of something outside ourself – a person, something in nature, even an object – or something inside us – feelings, longings, thoughts, sensations – all simply wants to be lovingly known. Spontaneous liberation. If human beings have any part to play in such a process of liberation it's surely through opening and allowing ourselves to be permeated by all that exists and strives for light and freedom both within us and in the world. It is as though the pores of our being were to open, and in that opening we may become permeated from within by what's deep and true. Not only that, but we also become open to the world, to experience, without defence and without preference. This opening to what's inside and what's outside becomes, I believe, a kind of transformative alchemy – transformative both of ourselves and of the world.

At the end of the Christian story Christ is taken up into heaven and is transfigured. On this point we're told in the gospel of St. Matthew that "his face did shine like the sun, and his raiment was as white as the light."[61]

What does this suggest? What could this mean once we strip this image of its religious associations and try and get at what the storyteller is attempting to convey?

It suggests to me that the oneness world can and does suffuse the twoness world. Furthermore, it does this not in some vague and rather general way. It does it in a very particular and powerful way. The oneness world can and does produce real effects in the twoness world. Real enough to turn matter into light, as in the story told in Matthew's gospel. Real enough that the coins or yarrow stalks used in an I Ching consultation will fall in precisely the appropriate way to highlight the details of a querent's situation. Real enough that the medical methodology that we know as homeopathy can produce healing results that clearly don't follow the laws of physics or chemistry characteristic of the spacetime world, and which according to twoness world logic shouldn't and couldn't be happening at all.

We humans in the twoness world have always called, through ritual and through prayer, for the guidance and succour of the oneness world. It may also be that there s an unfolding through time of the oneness world in the twoness world, in which the appearance and activity of the oneness world in the twoness world becomes progressively more specific, concrete and real.

This, then, is what it means to say that there is an unfolding or flowering of oneness in twoness. Oneness itself isn't conditioned by spacetime. Oneness is the potentiality, and in fact all potentialities. In twoness we see extension in time and space of possibilities. We might think of this unfolding of oneness in twoness as a kind of marriage between oneness and twoness, like the "mystical marriage" spoken of in Christian mysticism and in alchemy.

13. Pattern and Choice

Everything that's been said so far leads us to consider a question that's preoccupied philosophers, scholars, scientists and mystics of both East and West for centuries – the question of free will and whether we really do have choice or not in the face of our human condition and conditioning. This is a big question, and any kind of binary answer will probably fail at the outset.

From the perspective taken in this book we can say we inhabit three worlds. First, we're subject to the physical laws of the twoness world. Our physical bodies react and adapt to gravity, light, sound, touch and so on. And our emotions are also informed by these experiences. Human development theories have told us how we're affected and shaped especially by our earliest bodily experiences.[62]

Second, we exist in a world characterised by synchronicity and instantaneous connections. I term this the intermediary world and have suggested that in a sense this world partakes of both oneness and twoness. Separate objects and events connect in a manner suggesting that in essence they're not separate at all. This world is also a kind of bridge between twoness and oneness. It's the world of ritual, the shaman, the healer, and sometimes the artist and scientist too. It may also be that in this world we are connected with each other, nature and cosmos in previously unsuspected ways – at least unsuspected in our modern post-enlightenment era.

In the twoness world our bodies are subject to the laws of physics articulated by Newton and Einstein. They are subject to the physical forces of life and the universe – gravity, light, pressure, heat and cold and more. Here in the intermediary world our bodies (along with nature as a whole) partake in a morphic or quantum world of instantaneous connections. Our experience of this world is still mediated through our bodies. There's a sensitivity here which allows us to 'read' and react or adapt to fields which aren't just individual.[63] Such fields would connect us to each other, to our communities and to our species. On a larger scale they could connect us to nature and cosmos. They could also connect us to ideas, to archetypes and to the future.

Humans may well have the ability to sense and adapt to morphic fields through a sensitivity and responsiveness mediated through sensations, feelings and images. Oracles such as the *I Ching* might use such channels – images and intuitions – to access our deep instinctual connection to the fields of nature, culture, the earth and cosmos. Artists and healers can do the same. They can naturally use such channels, or they can learn to.

Third, we come to the oneness world, the unbroken whole. In this realm all dualities disappear. Modern exemplars of this space such as Ramana Maharshi try to guide us to an experience of a universal consciousness beyond any notion of a separate self. Here even a notion of oneness is no longer useful. The sages simply say of this experience it is *advaita*, meaning *not-two*.

From this perspective, everything that's been said about the twoness and intermediary worlds becomes relative. In a sense they are simply ripples that come and go in the vast and ultimate emptiness. A similar description of the ultimate reality can be found in the Western mystical tradition too. Right at the start of the Book of Genesis we find: "And the earth was without form, and void; and darkness was upon the face of the deep. And the Spirit of God moved upon the face of the waters."[64] I love this poetic description of ultimate formlessness, and the origin of movement/form within it.

Ramana Maharshi is yet more explicit, pointing to the discovered fact that this isn't only a description of the ultimate nature of *it*, but of *you* as well. For since this reality is non-dual, then it and you cannot be different. This is the reported experience of the great sages such as Ramana. Even if this isn't my direct experience, can I intuit that this might be so, and allow for this possibility? How would this intuition inform my thinking and perception? Certainly questions of choice and free will would look very different from this perspective. If ultimately all will, all desire, all wishing is the movement of the One, what is our experience of choice then? We might say, paradoxically, that the realised individual has total freedom and none at all. Or put another way, you have realised the presence of undivided oneness in which your will becomes identified with the will or movement of the whole.

These are subtle questions in the face of which one's thought processes and attempts at linguistic expression constantly break down and come to nothing.

Character, destiny and fate in practice

Perhaps we can view all this in less black and white terms. We can say that the twoness world, obeying the laws of physics discovered by Newton and Einstein, is choiceless. Certainly Newton's classical physics describes a deterministic universe. Here, if you know all the forces at work down to the finest detail, you can accurately predict the course of all physical processes.

No quantum uncertainty here. There are only the laws of gravity, light, attraction and repulsion and so on. On the other hand, in the non-dual reality known by contemplatives throughout history all questions of choice or no choice are transcended by the one reality.

Probably most of us struggle somewhere on the spectrum between these opposites. We constantly find ourselves between the urge to dissolve into the one on the one hand, and the urge to retain our personhood on the other. This fundamental polarity in our nature gives rise to all kinds of psychological drives and complexities in our relationships with ourselves, others and the world. We're all somewhere on a spectrum between wanting to be part of or merged and wanting to be individual and separate.

Perhaps the Greek philosophers of the past can help us here with their closely related ideas of character (from the Greek, meaning "I engrave"), fate and destiny. All these terms suggest a preordained pattern working itself out in spacetime. This destiny or fate could be like the attractor we discussed earlier. Something from the future drawing us to some kind of individuation or completion. We are of course conditioned by elements in our past – experiences and memories. But philosophers in the past understood that there's also something in our own future, shaping us, informing us, calling us.

It may be that we have past conditioning we can do something about. We can work on it, seek help and healing. But beyond that there's something, a pattern, which is more fundamental, appearing as destiny or fate. As far as my existence in spacetime goes, it's my shape, my manner of being, my rhythm, my predisposition. Viewed from this perspective my life might look more like a destiny, or a pattern that is working itself out, is drawn towards its own destination, whether I agree with it or not.

Perhaps real choice consists more in finding out what this destiny, this pattern, wants. Where am I going? What meaning is trying to unfold through my life? From this perspective we might talk in terms more of surrender or submission to something mysterious within us. Something only partially known. Something only partially knowable. But something that is nevertheless carrying me, prompting me, leading me, guiding me.

From this perspective, choice could be more like a movement arising from oneness. (Think of Bohm's proposal of the holomovement as the basis of reality.) This isn't the choosing of a separate, fabricated self. It's a creative movement that responds to, rather than reacts to, the conditions of life. Furthermore, this movement would not appear until it was, as it were, needed. Just as in quantum mechanics all possibilities remain open until, under the act of observation, a particular constellation of reality is 'chosen' – the enigmatic quantum wave function collapse – so nothing is pre-structured here. From this perspective, choice can be seen as a creative act. It comes out of the moment. It isn't defined by the past. It is a response, not a reaction.

Considering the nature of choice in this light we could think more in terms of harmony or following or guidance. We could reimagine choosing to be more like a flow or a dance that arises in the oneness world. Think of a river flowing between its two banks. When we try and choose from a position in the twoness world, it s like being on one bank or the other. We choose the best bank and hope to avoid the other. We carry on hoping that our one-sided choices will bring us happiness. Sometimes they do and sometimes they don't. But such happiness, if it is acquired at all, will always be conditional. However we got it, whether with ease or difficulty, we can certainly easily lose it again. Such is the unpredictability of our lives. But choosing from the position of the oneness world is more like choosing from no-position. It would be more like attending to the flow and guidance of the river itself, and following that.

This sounds easier than it is. To attend to flow and guidance doesn't only mean letting go. It also requires that I cultivate openness, sensitivity and restraint. It means relaxing around my own position and my own opinions. It means being sensitive to the energy, needs and direction of the other or the group or situation. It means flexibility. Not knowing first, not knowing best. Neither is it excessive passivity. It means acting proportionally when action is called for, and holding back when it isn't, even if that means restraining an impulse to act. And once we commit to the flow of the river, we don't know where or how this movement will carry us. Maybe we can try and listen. Try to be aware. Try to trust.

Just to make this switch in our attitude is a relief. Just to stop seeing ourselves as the agency for everything that happens in our lives is a relief. This isn't to say I experience myself as a victim either. Agent and victim are the two ends of the very same delusion – the notion of a separate self as an object in a world of objects. But I could see myself as a participant in an unfathomable mystery. I could put down the burden of thinking that things are down to me. Then I needn't carry the crushing weight of the responsibility of it going wrong or failing. I can also relieve myself of the troublesome euphoria that follows on things going right and succeeding. I don't have to live in the world of swinging opposites with its inevitable round of disappointment or suffering.

In the next chapter we'll come back to the body again.

14. Body as Movement

"All entities move and nothing remains still." So said Heraclitus two and a half thousand years ago – a Greek philosopher exactly contemporaneous with Confucius, and whose philosophy makes one wonder whether he actually encountered the *I Ching*!

It seems we sometimes experience our bodies as objects, or at least think of them as such. And bodies are like objects in as much as they are subject to twoness world laws such as gravity. Ponder on your earliest experiences as an infant. How might you have experienced touch, pressure, weight, light or sound? How were you handled? Roughly, gently? Did you fall? These are our formative experiences of the sometimes hard facts of spacetime. And these experiences we now know very quickly shape our emotional experience and attitudes to the world.

But as Heraclitus said, nothing is static. So perhaps we started not as a fixed object but as a field of awareness. A field that we experienced as constant change and flux. What we might have wanted then, above all else, was some kind of certainty. As we developed we needed to know we'd be safe, warm, fed. No wonder we craved certainty. Our lives really depended on a degree of reliability.

So that inner experience of flux and change began to be crystallised. We began to recognise, and later on as we developed, to name, the experiences that were good because they meant we were getting what we needed, and the experiences that were bad, because we weren't. This, in a few sentences, is the story of our early development. We gradually, through survival necessity, tried to control or fix our environment.

As we developed further it became necessary to apply the same constraints to our inner environment. We soon realised that in order to get what we needed and wanted we were better off inhabiting the good and acceptable 'me' and in one way or another steering clear of the bad unacceptable me which wasn't so successful at getting our needs met. In a sense, we began to objectify our environment and ourselves. This complex process is well mapped in such psychological theories as *object relations theory*, in developmental psychologies such as Jung's and many others, and as a matter of fact in human development maps found in other disciplines such as homeopathy.

So what was fluid and changeable becomes gradually more constrained and fixed. Experience might, over time, become categorised into boxes. There's nothing wrong with categorisation. In fact, our capacity to name, to conceptualise and later to categorise is of the profoundest importance for our human development. Without it we couldn't survive or manipulate our environment. Beyond that we wouldn't be able to reflect on ourselves and our world. The further reaches of knowledge and understanding, from practical matters to the deepest spiritual insights, would all be impossible. Again, the question is how might we benefit from our linguistic and conceptualising abilities without losing flow, flexibility and adaptability?

As I've noted elsewhere this fixing can become a stuckness in the natural ebb and flow of bodily function.[65] As far as our health is concerned we can say that stuckness finds expression in the dysfunctions lying at the root of disease. Bodily systems get stuck in faulty habits and lose something of their flow. For example, a normal reaction such as accelerated breathing and constriction of the chest in the face of a threatening or frightening situation might become a tendency to habitually go into that reaction in a situation of minor or imagined stress. One becomes asthmatic. What was once normal and necessary becomes abnormal and unnecessary. Internal cyclic rhythms in body systems and functions lose their open, flowing and responsive character, becoming less adaptable and more fixed.

Any truly holistic medical or healing system must recognise and address such changes, and especially the inner causes of such changes, if it is to help someone to be well. Put simply, to free outer stuckness (physical ill-health) it's necessary to loosen the inner stuckness that shows up in our habits of thinking, feeling and reacting. What's inside shows up sooner or later on the outside. This holistic view is intrinsic to healing systems such as homeopathy.

In a slightly different approach, movement practitioners are interested in all aspects of the body's movement. Just as our inner experience was originally one of motion and change, so there was natural flow and movement for the body. Flow and natural cycle, or lack of it, is present in our cognition, in our internal body systems and in our bodily movement. The important question becomes: is this flow or rhythm ordered or disordered? And can our capacity to name, to think and to conceptualise exist in the flow so that we're neither too hard nor too soft, neither too fixed nor too flexible?

Some physical practices can liberate a sense of presence or flow in movement – sport, playing music, dance, tai chi. Another approach is non-stylised movement (or non-formal movement, so called to contrast with formal movement practices like yoga and tai chi). This is the approach I want to include here.

Non-formal movement practices such as Amerta movement have been written about elsewhere.[66] But I'll say a little here. Engaging in free (non-stylised) movement practice and consciously attending to the body as movement, might help us to be less defined by fixed positions. In such a practice, movement and noticing go together. We move, we pause and we notice. We allow ourselves to be open to what's in us and around us. But the movement helps to keep the noticing flexible too. We receive what's here and what's there, but we don't build a position from this noticing.

Fixed positions of attitude and point of view, with their accompanying predictable and habitual behaviours and actions, might become less dominant. This doesn't mean that one has no position, no form. But in movement practice position and form become more like snapshot moments in a sequence of movement. I can take a position when I need to, with integrity and commitment. But that position needn't become my fixed reality. I can do this in my movement practice, and I can practise this in my life.

Doodle suggesting a relationship between movement and position: *in movement practice this suggests points, pauses or positions – and even the coming and going of sensations, feelings and images – in a person's line of movement. This reminds us that in the quantum mechanical description of nature, things can be both wave and particle. Objects are said to be in a superpositional state until, in the act of measurement, the wavefunction of all measurement result possibilities collapses as a particle with specific measured values of location, momentum or spin. By way of analogy we can imagine non-formal movement practice as embracing both a wave-like or 'spread-out' quality of potential and possibility (implicate order) as well as a quality of locality and definite position (explicate order).*

A fixed position – fixed attitudes and habits, rooted in the experience of the body as a separate object in space – allows for little outside itself. The timeless and spaceless needs to appear in a time and in a space. But that time and place – none other than our physical reality here and now – needs to be solid *and* flexible. Needs to be grounded *and* able to receive. Or, solid and grounded *so* that it may receive. When we experience the body as movement we're not denying the reality of our physical presence in space. We're here. We're real. We're capable of taking a position, capable of perseverance, capable of doing what needs to be done, but not limited or fixed by those capacities. We are structured, but in a manner that's fluid, dynamic and capable of adaptation and change. This then gives us the capacity to be open to, available to, oneness – that which is beyond space and time and yet the source of creativity and inspiration in spacetime. Presence, free of history, free of agenda, can, given the space, show up in the here and now.

In the next two chapters we reflect on oneness again, before returning in the final chapter to science.

15. Emptiness and Fullness

To say that the oneness world is formless or empty doesn't go nearly far enough. Remember that the oneness world has been seen as the source of all. Although empty and without form, it has creative potential. Oneness, in so much as it reveals its potential through the intermediary world, is creative and causal. The fact that in wisdom traditions there's said to be a creative or causal source of our experienced reality gives us a clue to the insights of the sages and philosophers of the past. It tells us that the oneness world is the source of all creativity and inspiration. In some traditions the emptiness behind everything is also known as the *pleroma*, the *fullness*. Fullness here doesn't mean full of things. It means full of potential. The oneness world is empty and, in the form of the intermediary world, full of potential at the same time.[67]

The oneness world doesn't consist of separate objects. It's a state of unity. I've spoken of it as a world for the sake of clarity but, of course, it is not an object, even though it's the source of all objects. If I were to talk of it, I would be an object describing another object. So we must consider the oneness world as a unified field or a field of unity, in which the I that attempts to describe it is simply the field reflecting on and describing itself. The oneness world cannot consist of separate object/events, cannot be an object/event, and cannot be perceived by a separate object/event. The oneness world can be likened to the space in which all objects appear. One could say it is formless space that is aware. The Sanskrit word *satcitananda* classifies the fundamental qualities of the oneness world. It means "existence, consciousness, bliss". These are the properties of the formlessness that underlies existence.

Our human relationship with the oneness world has, via the intermediary world, been the central preoccupation of art, science and religion for thousands of years. Few have more simply described this relationship than the Sufi poet and mystic Rumi:

Out beyond ideas of wrongdoing and rightdoing,
there is a field. I'll meet you there.
When the soul lies down in that grass
the world is too full to talk about.
Ideas, language, even the phrase 'each other'
doesn't make any sense. [68]

16. Love and Wholeness

It might seem from everything that's been said here that the oneness world is entirely benign and that its appearance in the twoness world is always kind and gentle like the attention of a loving parent. If we think like this it could induce a kind of sleepiness and we could be in for a shock. The appearance of the oneness world can also be terrifying. It can inspire awe. It can make us shake. That's why God, in the old Testament of the Bible is referred to as an *awful* presence. The oneness world, the creative source, if not listened to, can be a stern teacher, or worse it can turn the order and predictability of our twoness world upside down.

According to ancient Chinese philosophy the oneness world (heaven) has the property of creative potential. The oneness world, although ultimately beyond form, is, through the intermediary world, the creative source. The symbol the ancients chose for this aspect of oneness was the dragon. The Chinese dragon could be in the heavens, or below in the earth. Either way it was a power not to be messed with but to be honoured and respected. If we don't honour the oneness world, in whatever form it appears to us in our twoness world, then the oneness world can make a lot of trouble for us. It can disrupt our life. It can make us ill. Why? Because the oneness world is the source of all. We cannot avoid it. It will appear in our life whether we like it or not.

Its purpose, if I can put it like this, is truth. The essential drive in us, in all life, is to be just what we are. The imperative of life, in whatever form it takes, is to be that which it is. This is the energy that drives life. This drive to be what we are cannot be stopped. Block it, suppress it, and it'll push back. Avoid it and it'll come through the back door – in our dreams, in our symptoms and even in our life situations. If we ignore it long enough it can actually be destructive. It is the power of the universe. It will unfold, come what may.

This understanding has been depicted in many ways in the myths and symbols that have come down to us from the distant past. For me a particularly potent symbol of the terrible and disruptive face of the oneness world is the card known as *The Tower* in the tarot pack. This card shows a medieval tower being struck by lightning.[69] As the lightning strikes and cracks the tower apart, two figures are thrown out. Could there be a more powerful symbol of the intervention of the oneness world, as the creative source, into a well-established twoness world? Or into a self that has grown grandiose, defended and out of touch. A self that has failed to bow to the wisdom of life, to a greater reality.

The creative can't be kept at bay. It can destroy outmoded forms. It can be a stern and troublesome teacher when we have ignored it for too long. What is this power that wants everything to fulfil its potential? That wants us to be real, to be true? Some name it love. Love wants all to be as it is. Wants everything, including you, to express its true nature. Therefore, love teaches wholeness. As Jung found, it is wholeness that opens the way. The necessity to include all that is shut out, all that has been denied, and yet craves light, warmth and recognition. Love is the way, wholeness the necessity.

17. Future Science

In this book I've placed quantum entanglement, synchronicity, similarity, homeopathy, morphic resonance and spiritual perspectives together on the page. Much as you might place pictures or sculptures near each other in a gallery, allowing you to walk around and amongst the exhibits, seeing them not only as individual objects but in relation to each other as well.

In so doing I haven't attempted to explain any one of them in terms of another. For example, I don't try to explain a healing practice such as homeopathy in terms of a scientific description of reality such as that advanced in quantum mechanics. Each of these fields of knowledge has its own approach and evidence base. Any attempt to explain one in terms of another quickly leads into difficulties and misunderstandings.

However, I have placed these different models and perspectives alongside each other, so we might be struck by the similarities or differences between them. In this way I've tried to point out the possible commonalities. I've tried, as it were, to build bridges between different islands.

I started with the birth of the modern scientific understanding of the world, with the findings of Newton and then Einstein. We saw how those understandings of the world were challenged by the advent of quantum physics, which demonstrated that an entirely objective view of the world – in which the observer, experimenter or experimental apparatus had no effect – was no longer possible. Heisenberg, Bohr and others showed that what you looked for and how you looked affected the outcome of your looking.

Quantum mechanics also demonstrated that, at the micro level, events could be related to each other – such as the correlated activity of two particles when one of the pair is measured – in the absence of any apparent causal mechanism which would account for the correlation. Quantum theory says that the state of a quantum particle (such as a photon) isn't determined until it is measured. And in the case of entangled particles the measurement of Particle A immediately determines the properties not only of Particle A but of Particle B as well.

The debate, sometimes heated, in scientific circles (Einstein, Bohr, Heisenberg, Pauli and others) concerning what would become known as quantum entanglement progressed through the 1920s and 1930s. It was often passionate and exposed entirely different understandings of how nature worked and what might or could be true. One question centred around whether action-at-a-distance, linking distant quantum particles, without any apparent causative mechanism was actually possible. It wasn't until the 1960s that John Bell showed that it *was* possible, and that attempts to show such connections were due to hidden variables – mathematical parameters that, although unknown and hidden from view, would nevertheless predetermine the activity of both particles – could not be empirically sustained.

Despite the fact that Bell's hypothesis has subsequently been experimentally proven, the debate concerning the facts of simultaneous correlation between particles has never really been settled. And in a sense it doesn't have to be. The predictions of quantum mechanics are so successful, allowing quantum laws to be employed in modern technology, that many scientists never need to bother themselves with the apparently strange and irrational facts that underpin these laws. They can just keep applying these laws in useful discoveries and technologies. Those who asked too many questions were encouraged, in the famous words attributed to Richard Feynman, to "shut up and calculate". So it appears that much of science – in the fields of biology and medicine for example – carries on as if the facts of quantum entanglement, lying at the heart of science, didn't exist. The belief that a demonstrable cause-and-effect reality is the only reality is still central to much scientific endeavour.

So where does this leave us? I've proposed a threefold model of oneness world, twoness world and intermediary world. I've tried to show that there's a precedent for such a view. I've drawn on understandings of reality from the past found, for example, in ancient Chinese philosophy expressed in the *I Ching*. I've also drawn on modern understandings such as physicist David Bohm's model of holomovement, implicate order and explicate order.

But where does the main body of scientists stand in relation to these proposals? Where does science, as it is currently formulated, stand? For the most part, and especially in popular science, science as currently understood is a science of the twoness world. It is extraordinarily successful at demonstrating, both theoretically and in terms of practical applications through technology, the laws and functions of the spacetime world.

But the unwritten presumption that pervades much of science is that only what can be explained by known scientific laws is real. Events that can't be explained by such laws, such as precognition, are not real. And those that maintain that they might be real are misled or even deceitful. As well as this it is maintained that all modern experimental evidence that could suggest that such events are real comes from experimental setups that are flawed, inadequate, and at best should be regarded as pseudoscience. The work of biologist Rupert Sheldrake referred to earlier is a good example. Mainstream scientists dismiss his work as pseudoscience and attempts are made to discredit him and his work, rather than looking at the facts with an open mind.[70] This by and large is the position of mainstream and popular science in the first quarter of the 21st century. The twoness world is real, measurable and demonstrable. Nothing else is.

So what about the oneness world and the intermediary world? Has science anything to say about these?

I've used the term oneness world to represent the unbroken and undivided reality at the root of all that exists. It's described in the world's spiritual traditions. Its reality is affirmed by mystics from Lao Tzu to Meister Eckhart. As such it really lies so far outside the domain of modern science that it poses no threat. Science and scientists can leave all this to religion and spirituality. In their private lives scientists can be religious or spiritual, or they can regard all that as illusion. Either way it leaves their scientific work largely unaffected. At best, scientists admit they don't know and therefore can't say anything for or against such descriptions. The problem, like the fact of quantum entanglement, is avoided.

Let's move on now to the question of the intermediary world. This could represent a yet bigger problem for modern science. When researchers show that experimenters might be able to predict the symbol on a card before the card is turned up, or that certain people know what will happen before it happens, or that thoughts can affect the shape and appearance of ice crystals, many scientists become wary and even defensive because if these things were shown to be true much of the rational basis of the modern scientific paradigm would be challenged (see note 31). The materialist world view fundamental to modern science would be threatened. Why does this matter so much to scientists? A comprehensive discussion of this point is beyond the scope of this book, but I'll make some basic proposals here.

I've suggested that the intermediary world is in a sense a bridge between the twoness world and the oneness world. It's that aspect of the oneness world, which although whole and undivided, contains all the potential and possibilities for apparently separate things and events in spacetime. The intermediary world is also the world of acausal and meaningful connections – connections that can have real effects in spacetime – that can't be explained by current scientific models.

According to contemporary science, events that defy a causal explanation, or synchronous events that might involve a subjective element, cannot be real because they cannot be explained by the laws of nature as understood by science. Science as we know it is extraordinarily good in the twoness world, in spacetime, but not in the world of non-local connections and not in the world of undivided unity. If a causal explanation can't be given, whatever observational or anecdotal evidence there might be, these things cannot be happening.

I have suggested that non-local and acausal connections could be a key characteristic of the presence of oneness in twoness. When objects and events in spacetime behave as if they're mysteriously linked – in other words separate objects and activities are immediately correlated without any known causal connection – we might think of this as undivided oneness appearing in twoness. The dimension of oneness that has the capacity to contain all possibilities for separate objects and events – what David Bohm classifies as the implicate order – partakes, as it were, both of the oneness world and the twoness world. It's the domain where separate objects and events are connected in a way that suggests they're only *apparently* separate from each other. Things can still be in a state of instantaneous knowing or connection with each other, across space and time.

In summary then, we have a kind of hierarchy of oneness, intermediary and twoness. Oneness is *causeless*, in the sense that oneness is a state of all-embracing unity transcending all difference and all causal relationships. Twoness is *causal* in the sense that separate objects and events are bound together by spacetime laws of cause and effect. And the intermediary is *acausal* in that apparently separate objects and events are linked in a manner defying causal explanation. There is oneness, intermediary and twoness. Or causeless, acausal and causal. The intermediary world can also be said to be the bridge between, or the interpenetration of, oneness and twoness, the causeless and the causal.

It is the intermediary world that is the biggest problem for modern science. Why? Because the intermediary world is one of phenomena that show up in this world, in spacetime, and must therefore be a legitimate object for scientific observation and theory. But, as we've seen, from the scientific perspective, this is a world of inexplicable events and connections. For scientists this means that these things aren't happening or are only imagined. Or it could mean that the prevailing scientific model of reality is incomplete – a possibility that many scientists would not be willing to entertain. Scientists would of course acknowledge the incompleteness of scientific knowledge of the twoness world. But the suggestion that there are whole areas of reality and experience lying outside the current scientific model would represent a much greater challenge.

So a fundamental problem for modern science is the possibility of acausal or non-local connections. And yet, as we've seen, embedded in the quantum mechanical description of nature lies the enigma of quantum entanglement and the apparent fact of acausal connection.

When it comes to the intermediary world, acausal connection isn't the only problem for modern science. The current scientific worldview also has a problem with subjectivity. And we've seen that acausal connections between subjective states and outer events are also a feature of the intermediary world. For example, in precognition there's a connection between my internal experience and the occurrence of outer events. The *I Ching* also employs such non-local connections between subjective states and outer events.

Why does science see subjectivity as such a problem? With the advent of the Enlightenment, scientific methodology, consisting of hypothesis and empirical experiment to prove or disprove the hypothesis, took the central ground. The discipline of observation of the natural world was of course not new. But science now became the dominant form of knowledge. And rightly so. The scientific method seeks to establish what is objectively true, regardless of the background, cultural conditioning, individual preferences and so on of a theoretician or experimenter. And today we see theories being proposed, challenged and tested in research institutions by groups or individuals from all round the world, unhindered by national, cultural and gender perspectives. Science is global and aims to transcend individual and cultural preferences and prejudices.

Science replaced the older mythic description of the world.[71] The mythic form of knowledge was symbolic and imaginational. It was also culture specific. All mythic cultures produced stories and myths that conveyed understanding of the world and which acted as unifying agents around which individual members of a society could coalesce. Even though it's been demonstrated by 20th-century scholars that common themes and images can be found in stories and myths originating in different parts of the world and from different historical periods, the fact remains that these descriptions of reality are deeply subjective.[72] For thousands of years, individuals, groups and cultures have been moved by, sustained and held by the great stories, such as creation myths, handed down to them from time immemorial. These powerful stories offer a particular kind of gateway to truth and understanding. A gateway that has more to do with an instinctual and imaginational recognition of truth than with the rational understanding valued by science.

As modern science gained influence with its quest for objective truth, it necessarily distanced itself from the older mythic understanding of the world, which was seen as unreliable and a source of delusion and superstition.

But something important has been lost in this apparent advance of knowledge. As Ken Wilber and others have shown, older forms of consciousness with their attendant ways of knowledge don't just disappear. Rather they sink below the surface and live on in the unconscious. As consciousness develops, progresses and widens, whether in a human individual or in the cultural history of the species, it is not enough simply to transcend what went before. That leads to suppression and all manner of consequent troubles.

In all streams of development that involve a progressive widening or elevating of consciousness, it is necessary to include what went before. The newer capacities must transcend *and* include the older capacities. And in human beings the older capacities are the seat of greater instinctual power and connection to life. They are shut out at the peril of the health of individual and cultural group.[73]

The overly rational man or woman can feel threatened by the more immediate and unpredictable worlds of feeling, emotion or instinct. Emotions and instinct don't give repeatable and reliable observational results. But emotionally and instinctually orientated people can be very accurate in their reading of people and situations. Rationality works through analysing the parts of something, the parts that make up the whole. The older cognitive capacities of emotion and instinct, being more closely connected with survival, can more easily read situations as a whole and can react immediately and accurately unencumbered by thought.

However, these older capacities are also self-referenced and unable to see beyond a limited perspective. As Wilber has comprehensively set out, these older capacities cannot, for example, give rise to global concern or notions of universal rights. Thus humans, in order to be truly human, are on the path of developing the higher faculties of rationality, and beyond that the more integrative and holistic capacities of consciousness. But if these higher more comprehensive capacities develop at the expense of the older, then the whole structure becomes top-heavy, unstable and in constant danger of collapse. We become uprooted from nature, divorced from our own origins, our own roots and our own bodies, often with disastrous consequences for our own physical or psychological health, as well as the health and well-being of our mother earth. Put simply, the one-sided development spoken of here threatens our survival as a species, because it produces an unsustainable way of life and unsustainable relationships to nature, the earth and each other. Yet once we become aware of this one-sidedness in our development we should also be careful not to undervalue the gift of rationality which has been so hard won, and is so important for our capacity to survive and to understand ourselves, each other and the world.

So where does this leave science and the legitimate modern scientific quest for objective truth freed from subjective bias and prejudice?

When quantum mechanics showed that the objective facts of the world might not be so completely objective after all it created deep divisions between the great physicists of the day. The way the world behaved might after all defy a rational cause-and-effect description. It might also be that the subjective states of humans in general and scientists in particular could play a part in the way the world worked. Despite being termed 'quantum mechanics', quantum physics seemed to be showing that the cosmos was not a machine after all! Life isn't mechanical. Things can be connected in the absence of cause-and-effect mechanisms, and subjectivity, or at least the presence of an observer, can influence experimental outcomes.

The presence of pattern

In parallel with the emergence of the new quantum mechanical description of nature, Jung was pioneering a new understanding of the human psyche. We don't know to what extent Jung's relationship with leading quantum physicist Wolfgang Pauli influenced the formulation of his theory of synchronicity. But we do know that Jung sought to show that events and people could be meaningfully connected in the absence of causal mechanisms that would account for those connections: for example, a person in one location knowing of something happening in another location in the absence of any known communication mechanism between the two sites. And if the knowing was of something yet to happen, this would indicate correlation between events not only separate in space, but in time also. Jung also proposed that such events are somehow "entangled" with each other in the presence of the subjective state of the participant in, or witness to, these events. Our subjective state plays a role and is part of such events.

It's possible that in synchronistic events a pattern is present that includes external events as well as the subjective state of an individual or a group. The pattern that links events that are separate in space, and possibly time as well, can somehow be inside us and outside at the same time. How might this come about?

According to Jung much within us that's in the dark wants to come into consciousness, into the light, where it can be known, accepted, befriended and can become part of our wholeness. These unconscious elements within us – unconscious but needing to become conscious – will find whatever channel they can for expression: channels like dreams and body sensations.[74] (It's important to remember that such elements relate not only to the parts of us that were repressed and wounded in the past and need to be healed or redeemed. There's also unrealised potential or undeveloped seeds of what we might be. Both the past and the future might desire and need our attention.)

So we can say that what can't for one reason or another become conscious shows up firstly and most easily in dreams. Dreams come when our more conscious cognitive functions are on pause. This gives a chance for feelings and reactions that are below the surface, in the twilight of the subconscious psyche, to make an entrance in the form of dream images and events. (In this sense dreams have a regulatory function.)

The body can also become the bearer of unconscious patterns. What if dreams are unheard or cannot be attended to? Then the unconscious must seek another channel. It might then express itself in the darkness of the body. This is particularly evident in childhood where the regulatory function of the unconscious will find outlet for thwarted energies and reactions through acute and sub-acute physical manifestations – fevers or skin conditions such as eczema for example. Thus unconscious patterns can imprint themselves in the world of dreams, and possibly in the sensations and functions of the body as well. Is there another channel available to the unconscious? Jung's researches into synchronicity suggest there is.

Jung, through his theory of synchronicity, proposed the presence of patterns which might not only show up simultaneously in our psychological and physical functioning, but might also link our inner world with the external world. These patterns, which he named *archetypes*, don't operate according to spacetime laws. They are in a sense beyond spacetime, but show up in spacetime in dreams, body states and sensations, and in synchronistic events as well.

Inner and outer can it seems, under certain conditions, interpenetrate and influence each other. A pattern can somehow be inside us, in our unconscious, in our dreams, as well as in the world around us. Such a pattern, undefined by spacetime laws, and perhaps acting as a kind of vortex, draws in or captures our awareness, our body sensations, and even life events of which we are a part. Such a pattern might also resonate with patterns found in nature – in atoms, DNA molecules, crystals, plants, animals and the movement of water or flocks of birds.

This idea of a pattern corresponds closely to Jung's term *archetype*. Archetypes are the universal patterns within typical human situations and perceptions. They show up especially in the images and symbols of the unconscious, as well as in instinctual behaviours common to all humans.

Archetypal patterns, themselves beyond direct perception or representation, can show up both physically and psychologically. As well as this they can be present simultaneously in both our inner and outer worlds. Jung sometimes used the term *psychoid* to refer to this latter property of archetypal patterns.[75] Curiously enough it is well recorded that Wolfgang Pauli, one of the most brilliant physicists of his day who worked closely with Jung, often produced what his friends and colleagues dubbed the "Pauli effect". He and his colleagues noted on frequent occasions that, when Pauli was present in a laboratory, equipment would malfunction in some way. People probably laughed about it and took it with a pinch of salt. But it was noted many times. There were also reports that the effect might happen when Pauli was some distance away, or that an inanimate object (such as a vase) could be affected, suggesting that such effects, if they were real, could not be readily put down to electromagnetic effects.

Jung's theory suggests that synchronistic events happen in the presence of a constellated archetypal pattern. When such a pattern is already, under certain conditions, activated and seeking expression through dreams and body states, it can become a 'carrier' of synchronistic events. We can also say that such a pattern, being both inside and outside us, is somehow activated or constellated by our own unconscious condition.

Physics and the intermediary world

Quantum objects can behave as particles or waves. Light can be a wave or particle (photon). And matter too can be a particle (electron) or a wave. Quantum objects seem to take on properties when measured or observed. When not observed they're said to only exist in a superpositional state. Quantum objects can also be linked with each other in the absence of any kind of signal passing between them. They can be entangled. All these properties of quantum objects have been experimentally verified, but only at the scale of the very small, in the world of photons and electrons.

But scientists are constantly pushing this boundary. At what scale can quantum attributes, such as being both wave and particle or being entangled, still be observed? So far quantum entanglement has been observed at larger scales only up to the size of small carbon molecules. Where is the boundary between the world of quantum physics where quantum rules apply, and the world of classical physics where classical rules apply? Classical physics deals with larger objects that maintain clearly defined attributes whether they're being observed or not. The classical world (the laws of which were formulated by Newton and Einstein) has objective existence independent of whether you are there or not. Or so it seems.

At this point you might wonder why larger objects such as stones or trees don't show the kind of quantum uncertainty that occurs at very small scales. Why don't stones or trees take on attributes during the act of observation or measurement, as quantum objects do? Why don't larger objects behave as waves or things, or both at the same time, just like quantum objects? Why aren't larger objects entangled with each other, just like quantum objects? Why doesn't a large object exist in a superpositional state where an attribute such as its position or its velocity isn't decided until it's observed (the collapse of the wave-function).

Well, can we be sure it doesn't? Can we be sure a stone or tree doesn't alter under the act of observation or being given attention? Still, even if a stone or a tree is altered at the quantum level when it's observed, its objective reality as an object out there, whether looked at or not, seems to remain. It remains classically defined.

We could suggest that, from a quantum mechanical perspective (and this might stretch speculation and imagination to the limit), this is because such an object, a tree for example, is always, so to speak, observed or witnessed. A tree is always present to something else, even if that something else is not human, but another tree or a wolf or the earth, or even an inanimate object such as a rock or measuring device. Thus it always sustains its attributes, because it is always witnessed.

This reminds us of the controversy between Einstein and quantum scientists such as Niels Bohr. Is there an objective reality independent of observation, measurement, witnessing, attention, or not? This opposition of ideas within science about reality has not been resolved to this day.

But back to trees and rocks – now from the perspective of morphic resonance. Is it possible that at the macro level, as opposed to the micro quantum level, objects hold their form and function through a kind of morphic habit? That they hold an habitual form and pattern of function through the activity of their morphic fields. This 'morphic habit' could allow a macro object like a tree to sustain form and function over time independent, to a certain extent anyway, of the effect of observation, measurement or attention.

This would mean that at the quantum level there would be a kind of flow in which sets of possibilities (quantum wave functions) were constantly collapsing into particles with measurable attributes. This activity would be held in a higher order morphic field. We can imagine this if we think of a picture made up of dots in which the dots are constantly popping in and out of existence, but still in the framework of the recognisable picture.

The Pine Tree at Saint Tropez: Paul Signac (1863-1935) – a painter of the pointillist school. (With apologies for using a black and white version of this famous 1909 painting.) Were Signac and other painters of the period in some way precognisant of developments that would take place in physics in the 1920s?

Science and the three worlds

Let's continue with this idea of a threefold reality. Our primary reality, our primary ground, is an unbroken whole, an undividedness. This reality is the one experienced and reported on by spiritual traditions and mystics in different times and cultures. Of course, this undividedness is not an object like other objects that can be experienced. Such objects can be external, trees or stones for example, or internal, thoughts for example. The oneness however is consciousness itself, or the space in which everything appears. It's a background that is somehow empty but also full of life and potential as well. Immensely still, immensely vibrant, immensely empty, and yet immensely full.

20th-century physicists in their observations of physical reality also seemed drawn to conclude that there might exist an underlying and completely unified reality. We've already considered Bohm's notion of the holomovement and the implicate order. Bohm also proposed, but was never able to prove, the existence of something he named the *pilot wave*. A wave that would instantaneously connect everything in the universe and would guide the activity of quantum particles. Bohm's theory of a pilot wave was part of his attempt to show that quantum particles might have real objective attributes independent of observation or measurement. Hidden variables might in fact account for the observed properties of particles. In this model the pilot wave guides the activity and instantaneous correlation of particles. It is capable of responding instantaneously to changes anywhere in the universe and communicating that change to a quantum object such as an electron, thus altering its location and momentum. However, in order to accomplish this, the wave's movement must be faster than light (superluminal). This possibility was already ruled out by Einstein's theory of general relativity which establishes that no wave or information can travel faster than light.

Mystics have described unbroken oneness as the ground of all being. They describe an inner experience in which all divisions such as inner and outer or subjective and objective disappear. Scientists on the other hand seek a single law, equation or wave that accounts for all phenomena. Mystics see from the inside and scientists from the outside. Mystics ask who is the witness, who is the experiencer? Scientists focus on what is experienced. A universal science would embrace both. It would recognise that consciousness is primary. All arises in consciousness. So we could say that, when scientists seek a unifying law of everything, this is a kind of reflection of the underlying unity that mystics have already experienced and described. Nevertheless, this unity is constantly unfolding into life. The implicate is constantly unfolding as the explicate. The underlying unity and the world are in fact an ever-unfolding unity which can be known both from within and without.

We also live in an apparent reality of separate objects and events. This is the spacetime world of cause and effect described by Newton, Einstein and modern science – the twoness world.

Between oneness and twoness we find ourselves in the less clearly defined intermediary world. The world of acausal instantaneous connections where inner and outer can be meaningfully intertwined. Here things and events, while appearing to be separate, show instantaneous connections and knowing. That things which appear to be separate can somehow be intimately connected with each other could point to an underlying non-dual reality. A reality of non-separability. A oneness.

Is it possible that an holistic science of the future could recognise and embrace this three-fold reality? It would recognise the oneness out of which everything comes. It would value and seek to understand the experiences and descriptions of a single all-embracing reality or consciousness reported by mystics from different traditions and different times.

It would also study spacetime and causal connections as it now does. However it would study acausal connections as well as causal spacetime laws. And it would also observe and try to understand the interpenetration of outer reality and inner subjective states.

An holistic scientist of the kind suggested here would seek to become aware of their own inner processes. They would seek to understand their own habits and projections. They would be especially interested in the prejudices and positional tendencies that might colour their understanding of external reality, and even affect the outcomes of experiment and observation. (On this last point they would also need to be especially aware of political and corporate business interests that could affect their freedom to pursue objective research unhampered by such external forces).

Such a scientist might go further. Their awareness of their inner world might only be a first step. In expanding their awareness as well as loosening the grip of habitual modes of thought, they might open up to an understanding and sympathy with other subjective experiences, besides their own. This sympathy might extend to the subjective experience of other humans. Even more radically it could extend to other species – to animals and plants. A science of the future could recognise and be in sympathy with the subjective world of plants and animals, and even of the earth and cosmos as well.

Perhaps there is a precedent for such a science. The *I Ching*, although arising from a culture far older than our own, and one that was of course mythically embedded (a culture held together through a mythic understanding of the world presented through story and symbol, and bound by strict observances and hierarchies), does nevertheless go some way to meeting the criteria outlined above. Chinese culture recognised the fundamental ground or oneness out of which everything arises – the Tao. It was also the repository for the then sum-total of knowledge deriving from the observation of cosmos, nature, and human society and culture. It included observations of nature recorded over hundreds and perhaps thousands of years – its own version of our modern science.

But their wisdom tradition went further. It included an understanding of the mysterious non-local connections that can exist between people and events or between people and nature.[76] In fact it enshrined this understanding in the use of the oracle as a means of finding direction in the daily matters of human life. From this perspective we might say it offered a complete map of reality.

In the modern world it may be that homeopathy occupies somewhat similar ground. Of course, homeopathy doesn't represent a universal map in the way the *I Ching* does. Rather it's a system of healing with a theoretical map and practical application. Homeopathy comprises a comprehensive body of data based on observations of the effects of medicinal substances on human beings. This data forms the basis for homeopathic practice. But it may also be that in the practice of homeopathy we see the use of relationships between ourselves and natural substances that aren't only causal but acausal as well. The action of homeopathic remedies may point to our existence not only in a causal world, but one of non-local, acausal connections as well.

In the 20th century Jung was also working towards a description of reality that would be more complete. After discussions with Pauli he proposed a map that "satisfies on the one hand the postulates of modern physics, and on the other hand those of psychology."[77]

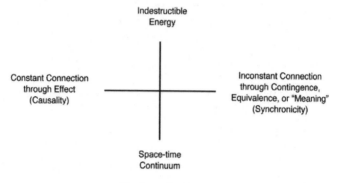

The Jung/Pauli map

In oneness the apparent division between inner and outer dissolves. In twoness the work of scientists depends on the objectivity and separation of the observer from what is observed – a view that was called into question with the advent of quantum experimental theory. In the intermediary world things that appear separate can also be in a kind of connection with each other as though they weren't fundamentally separate at all.

There's another important point. Trying to describe or account for one world from the perspective of another can lead to confusion. For example, when scientists try to account for spiritual experiences by invoking the known laws of modern science this usually leads nowhere, neither proving nor disproving anything. Laws governing one world might not be true in others.

Twoness is governed by scientifically known laws of cause and effect and action and reaction. But these laws don't necessarily hold up in the intermediary world, the world of instantaneous and meaningful correlations where subjective experience and objective fact might in some way interpenetrate. Confusion arises when scientists try to apply the laws of twoness to the intermediary world. So when scientists who believe the laws of twoness are the only real laws hear of events that defy these laws they often stop inquiring and trying to find out. Events such as precognition are said to be impossible (because no causal mechanism can be demonstrated) and therefore not worthy of honest investigation.

Both these worlds exist in oneness – a reality that transcends and includes intermediary and twoness worlds. This really isn't a world at all, but a state of consciousness in which transcendent unity is experienced. From here the whole material world including all its scientifically verified laws are seen as a kind of projection of consciousness, a consciousness both universal and transcendent as well as individual and immanent.

Following on from the Jung/Pauli map, I add my own maps.

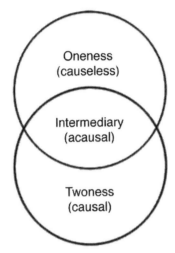

This map suggests a hierarchical reality of three orders. Each order (world) might transcend and include the previous order (twoness is transcended by, and included in, the intermediary world, which in turn is transcended by, and included in, oneness).

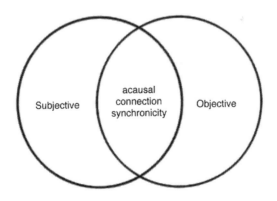

This map points to the interpenetration of our subjective reality and the objective world.

When we look at different areas of human activity we can see that such activities are really fields of activity or inquiry especially rooted in one or another of the three realms:

Oneness World	Intermediary World	Twoness World
Causeless	Acausal	Causal
Alocal	Non-local	Local
Transcends connection or disconnection	Acausal connection	Causal connection
Timeless	Instantaneous connection (not limited by spacetime)	Time delay in connection (defined by speed of light)
Transcends duality of subject and object	Subjective human states (as well as non-human subjective states of animals, plants etc.?) are involved in connections	Connections occur independently of human or other forms of witnessing consciousness
Mystic	Artist, shaman, healer, theoretical scientist	Practical scientist, engineer, craftsman

What areas of human knowledge and activity correspond to each of these worlds? The oneness world is the world of the mystic – the person who contemplates and directly experiences underlying oneness. The intermediary world is the world of artists, shamans, healers and theoretical scientists. The women and men who bring the invisible into the visible. Those who reach beyond spacetime but produce an effect in spacetime. The twoness world is the natural home of scientists, engineers and craftsmen – those who must understand and apply the laws of spacetime.

A new holistic science would continue to observe life and formulate laws as it now does. However, this activity would take place against the background of knowledge of and profound respect and gratitude to the unbroken whole lying behind all inward and outward events. A new science would recognise how outwardly separate things and events could be acausally connected with each other within a background of oneness (see illustration on next page). It would also recognise the possibility of acausal connection between the inner life of a human being and outer events. Such connections, having no demonstrable cause-and-effect relationship, could be held in a non-local pattern itself not defined by spacetime. A new science would especially try to understand the patterns that underlie all aspects of inner and outer life.

Bringing these elements together in a single model is fraught with difficulty, not least of which is our own capacity to believe things that make us feel happy and secure, but which might not be true. The tendency to ignore anything, including evidence, that challenges our often precarious hold on ourselves and our reality is widespread and even ubiquitous.

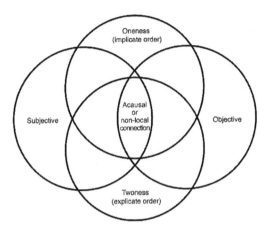

Do we have the capacity to keep our hearts and minds open as we build provisional structures of knowledge – theoretical models that at any time may be shown, in the light of further experience, research and evidence, to be true or untrue – within the vast mystery of the unknown, and perhaps unknowable?

Notes

Chapter 1

[1] Carlo Rovelli, 2006, *Seven Brief Lessons On Physics*, Penguin Books, p.6

[2] ibid. p.6

[3] ibid. p.8

[4] Nick Strobel, '*Nick Strobel's Astronomy Notes*, www.astronomynotes.com

Chapter 2

[5] Marianne Freiberger, 'Physics in a minute: the double slit experiment' www.plus.maths.org, 5 Feb. 2017

[6] Marianne Freiberger, 'A ridiculously short introduction to some very basic quantum mechanics', www.plus.maths, 19 May 2016

[7] See also: Bernard Carr, 'Physics of the Observer', YouTube, 9 Oct. 2017

[8] 'Does the quantum wave function represent reality?', www.phys.org, 25 Apr. 2012

[9] Nick Herbert, 1985, *Quantum Reality: Beyond the new physics*, Anchor Books p.49

[10] ibid. pp.49-50

[11] ibid. p.188-9

[12] There are several popular readership books on the subject. Louisa Gilder, 2009, *The Age of Entanglement: When quantum physics was reborn*, is an entertaining account of the development of quantum mechanics and quantum entanglement, and of the personal conversations and relationships between the physicists involved.

Nick Herbert's *Quantum Reality: Beyond the new physics* is a more metaphysical account, which leads to a far-reaching interpretation of quantum physics that is in keeping with ideas expressed in this book, but dismissed by some physicists as unwarranted metaphysical speculation.

Chapter 3

[13] C.G. Jung, 1960/2010 *Synchronicity: An acausal connecting principle*, Princeton University Press

[14] For the full scarab beetle story, along with Jung's comments, see Jung, 1960/2010, pp.108-110. Jung tells us that the beetle story is only one amongst many such incidents in his experience. I want to mention here two further stories concerning birds.

The first is again reported by Jung. A woman told him that at the deaths of both her mother and grandmother a number of birds had gathered outside the windows of the death-chamber. Later her husband was sent to a consultant with "some apparently quite innocuous symptoms" and was told there was no cause for concern. However on the way home he collapsed and was brought home dying. His wife was, on his arrival, already in a great state of anxiety because soon after her husband had gone to the consultant a whole flock of birds had landed on their house. "She naturally remembered the similar incidents that had happened at the death of her own relatives and feared the worst." (op. cit. p 22)

Another strange story concerning birds was told to me by a student of Javanese movement teacher and performance artist, Suprapto Suryodarmo (1945-2019). Prapto, as he was known, would sometimes give a cryptic instruction to a movement practitioner that could, as it were, speak to their inner being rather than rational understanding. My new acquaintance told me that she had always had a connection with birds. On one occasion she was attending a workshop with Prapto, who said to her "you are a master of flying...please give us an offering or ritual on *the nest of the bird.*"

When she returned home and to her daily movement practice, a bird appeared at the window of her movement studio and, when she paid no attention to it, knocked on the window. It appeared every day at the same time for the next month. It never appeared at other times of the day when someone else was using the studio. One day after a month she went to her car and found a dead bird (not the same bird) on the passenger seat. There was no indication as to how the bird might have got in. After this incident the bird that had been coming to her studio window no longer appeared.

In both these examples we can easily appreciate a possible subjective element to the events reported. We might say that in both cases, as I discuss in Chapter 3, the unconscious of the subject is constellated: such synchronistic events don't take place on neutral ground, but rather in particular 'charged' circumstances (death of family members and working on a meaningful level with a movement teacher). We can say that in both cases a pattern that incorporates inner responses and outer events was activated.

[15] C.G. Jung, op. cit. p.99

[16] ibid. p.100

[17] ibid. pp.100-1

[18] For a scholarly survey of placebo studies, see: Daniel Moerman, 2002, *Meaning, Medicine and the 'Placebo Effect'*, Cambridge University Press

For popular works on placebo and healing, see:
Joe Dispenza, 2014, *You Are The Placebo: Making your mind matter*, Hay House
Bruce H. Lipton, 2005, *The Biology of Belief*, Hay House

[19] ibid. pp.102-3

Chapter 4

[20] C.G. Jung, 1968, *Psychology and Alchemy* (Collected works, volume 12), Routledge and Kegan Paul, p.301

[21] Arthur I. Miller, 2009, *Deciphering the Cosmic Number: The strange friendship of Wolfgang Pauli and Carl Jung*, W. W. Norton and Co., p.201. Miller notes the source of this quote in his annotations to the text, p.298.

[22] For more detailed explanations, discussions and examples of morphic fields, morphogenetic fields and morphic resonance, see: www.sheldrake.org.

[23] Rupert Sheldrake, 1989, *The Presence of the Past*, Fontana, p.112

[24] ibid. p.109

[25] ibid. p.302

[26] ibid. p.35

[27] ibid. p.304

[28] ibid. pp.35-36

[29] It's of interest and a matter of record that Jung knew about the principle of similarity in homeopathy as well, although he never, as far as we know, mentioned this knowledge in public. Edward Whitmont, the well-known Jungian analyst and homeopath mentioned in chapter 5, knew Jung personally. Dr. Whitmont told me that he spent two hours explaining the philosophy and practice principles of homeopathy to Jung. Jung listened attentively and without interruption for the two hours. He asked no questions, and the subject was never mentioned again (*personal conversation between the author and Dr. Whitmont*). Whitmont is known for a number of books on Jungian analysis, healing, dreams and homeopathy. For example, *Return of the Goddess*, 1983; *Psyche and Substance*, 1980; *The Alchemy of Healing*, 1993; *Dreams, a portal to the source* (with Sylvia Brinton Perera), 1989.

Chapter 5

[30] For more on the history of similarity in healing and medicine see:

Elizabeth Danciger, 1987, *The Emergence of Homeopathy: Alchemy into medicine*, Century Hutchinson

Edward Whitmont, 1993, *The Alchemy of Healing: Psyche and soma*, North Atlantic Books

[31] There is strong and growing evidence that water is a mysterious and plastic substance capable of 'memory' of substances that were once present in it but have since been diluted away, as well as retaining the effects of mechanical or electromagnetic influences that it has been subjected to. It is suggested that once a substance present in the water, such as molecules of DNA, has been diluted away, certain nanostructures formed by the original presence of the substance are retained. There is also evidence to suggest that these nanostructures can hold electromagnetic charges similar to those emitted from the original DNA material that was diluted. Gerald Pollack has produced evidence for the structuring capacity of water, which has a crystalline form when in contact with surfaces such as a container or the surfaces of solutes within the water. Water can also absorb radiant energy, for example from the sun. This doesn't simply result in heat, but means water can produce chemical, optical, electrical and even mechanical energy. "Water, therefore, acts as a transducer, absorbing one kind of energy and converting it into other kinds. The conversion may occur instantaneously, as in fluorescence, or it may get held in reserve for future use." (Gerald Pollack, 2013, *The Fourth Phase of Water*, Ebner and Sons, p.119)

Scientist Jacques Benveniste became famous for his experiments in which white blood cells release histamine when exposed to an immunoglobulin antibody. What was shocking was his claim that even when the antibody was serially diluted, the resulting solution was still able to evoke the histamine response, as though the antibody was still there, when the physical presence of the antibody had been completely removed. The effect was only achieved when the water was shaken energetically during the procedure. The term memory-in-water was born. Following Benveniste's work, leading HIV researcher and Nobel laureate Luc Montagnier produced evidence to show that DNA from certain bacterial and viral species emitted electromagnetic signals in the form of low frequency electromagnetic waves (radio waves). When the same DNA was subject to high dilution and agitation (similar to homeopathic potentising procedure) it still produced electromagnetic signals. Montagnier noted that these dilutions couldn't contain any of the original organic material. But he also noted that these signals were only present up to dilution 10^{-18}.

There's plenty on the web on the work of Benveniste and Montagnier, e.g.: 'Electromagnetically Activated Water and the Puzzle of the Biological Signal', www.tcm.phy.cam.ac.uk

'DNA Sequence Reconstructed from Water Memory', www.i-sis.org.uk

The evidence for memory in water comes from rigorous research by serious scientists. It is nevertheless considered as pseudoscience by the orthodox scientific community. However, I choose to give serious consideration to the findings of Benveniste, Montagnier and others. (As a footnote on Benveniste's work with special relevance to proposals concerning non-local connections advanced in this book, I note the following point that was observed during attempts at replication of the Benveniste experiment: "Using the same experimental devices and setup as the Benveniste team, they failed to find any effect when running the experiment. Several 'positive' results were noted, but only when a particular one of Benveniste's researchers was running the equipment. 'We did not observe systematic influences such as pipetting differences, contamination, or violations in blinding or randomization that would explain these effects from the Benveniste investigator. However, our observations do not exclude these possibilities.' Benveniste admitted to having noticed this himself. 'He stated that certain individuals consistently get digital effects and other individuals get no effects or block those effects.'" *Water Memory*, Wikipedia)

Evidence for another, even stranger, class of memory-in-water comes from a variety of sources including the Japanese researcher Masaru Emoto, who has conducted many experiments in which water is exposed to influences such as thoughts, words or music. The experiments, which involve freezing the water samples, seem to show very different types of crystals being formed under the different influences. For example, water that's been exposed to the music of Bach, Mozart or Beethoven shows more beautiful crystals than water that's been exposed to heavy rock, which produces a less pleasing, more distorted crystal. He also conducted many experiments to show the effect of different words. Words that are loving or supportive produce well-formed or beautiful crystals, whereas words that produce negative emotions such as hatred, will produce crystals that are ugly or malformed. For more on the work of Masaru Emoto, see for example: 'Water the Great Mystery', YouTube

[32] Julian Carlyon, 2003, *Understanding Homeopathy, Homeopathic Understanding: Foundations of homeopathic philosophy and practice*, Helios Homeopathy

Chapter 6

[33] For a history of ideas in quantum biology from Bohr in the 1920s to the present day see: University of Surrey, *Quantum Biology – explained by Jim Al-Khalili*, YouTube, 12th May 2020

[34] Mae-Wan-Ho, 2008, *The Rainbow and the Worm*, World Scientific Publishing, p.284

[35] ibid. p.285

Here are some additional notes on wave coherence and decoherence, especially quantum coherence and decoherence:

Interference: "A fundamental property of waves, discovered by Thomas Young in the early years of the nineteenth century. When a wave interferes destructively with itself, its peak and trough cancel each other out: the result is flat water, an acoustic dead zone, or unexpected darkness or absence. Waves interfere constructively when two peaks coincide, creating a wave bigger than the sum of their heights." (Louisa Gilder, 2009, *The Age of Entanglement: When quantum physics was reborn*, Vintage Books, p.340)

For waves to interfere they have to be coherent.

Coherence and Decoherence: "A property of waves or wavefunctions, roughly defined as behaving as if the waves came from a single source. Adding together two coherent waves gives a clear interference pattern; adding together two incoherent waves gives a rapidly shifting pattern that smears out and becomes indistinct. The process of 'decoherence' destroys the coherence between two waves from a single source through random and fluctuating interactions with a larger environment." (Chad Orzel, 2010, *How to Teach Quantum Physics to your Dog*, Oneworld Publications, pp.271-2)

Quantum Coherence: Specifically, quantum coherence contemplates a situation where an object's wave property is split in two, and the two waves coherently interfere with each other. Quantum coherence is based on the idea that all objects have wave-like properties. It's in many ways similar to the concept of quantum entanglement, which involves the shared states of two quantum particles instead of two quantum waves of a single particle. (www.techopedia.com)

Because coherence or entanglement between quantum waves or particles can only be experimentally shown occurring in an environment free from external 'noise', physicists until now have not believed or have been unable to show that entanglement/coherence occurs at a macro scale such as in the human body. However some physicists believe that nature uses entanglement/coherence at scales larger than quantum particles and are looking to demonstrate how this might be possible. See: note 62.

Chapter 7

[36] David Bohm, 1995, *Wholeness and the Implicate Order*, Routledge, p.124

[37] ibid. p.151

[38] ibid. p.155

[39] ibid. pp.124-5

[40] Nick Herbert, op. cit., pp.214-5

[41] ibid. p.230

[42] David Bohm, op. cit., p.149

Chapter 8

[43] Perhaps the greatest genius of the *I Ching* is the way it has, over centuries, built a bridge between our more recently evolved rational capacities and the older levels of our psyche. These evolutionarily older levels are more embedded in nature and express themselves in an archaic language of symbols. The archaic psyche speaks the language of nature and is more closely connected with instinct, survival and the ability to be part of nature – to be natural.

The *I Ching* is a mathematical divinatory system that allows our older 'natural' self to speak to our modern more differentiated, but also more uprooted, self. This benefits both parties. Our modern, differentiated self maintains its roots in, and receives guidance from, nature, while our archaic natural self benefits from the light of modern (evolutionarily speaking) human awareness. With this awareness we can bring light into that part of us that has evolved in the womb of nature over millions of years.

Why would our ancient natural self need or benefit from this light of consciousness? One answer is that, as humans, we need to be natural but somehow also not defined by nature. When we look at animals and plants we see that individual species express patterns of growth, living and survival without self-reflection. That is their strength and their beauty. It's also their weakness because their capacity to adapt to environmental conditions is limited. Human individuals, on the other hand, can be part of nature but conscious of nature and conscious of a larger reality as well. They have the capacity, or at least the potential, for more scope than animals – more ability to take account of a bigger picture and to change as circumstances demand.

We might go further and suggest that human awareness is the means by which nature as a whole becomes self-aware. From this perspective this is the human function within nature. This process of nature becoming self-aware might be, as suggested in this book, itself a kind of transformative process within nature.

[44] *The I Ching or Book of Changes*, 1968, trans. Richard Wilhelm, foreword C. G. Jung, Routledge and Kegan Paul, pp.318-9

[45] Nigel Richmond, *The I Ching Oracle*, p.6, available as a PDF at: www.biroco.com/yijing/richmond.htm

[46] Gia-fu Feng and Jane English, 1989, *Lao Tzu: Tao Te Ching*, Vintage Books

[47] For a comprehensive overview of literature, studies and theories on human developmental see:

- Ken Wilber, 1995, *Sex, Ecology, Spirituality*, Shambhala
- Ken Wilber, 1996, *A Brief History of Everything*, Newleaf
- Julian Carlyon, op. cit. chapter 3

[48] D.C. Lau, 1963, *Lao Tzu: Tao Te Ching*, Penguin, chapter 1

Chapter 9

[49] C.G. Jung, 1960/2010 *Synchronicity: An acausal connecting principle*, Princeton University Press, p.102

[50] As has already been noted I don't see that a causal explanation of events would necessarily eliminate an acausal one. They could co-exist. In Jung's anecdote of the beetle there could have been a causal explanation for the beetle's behaviour – the temperature gradient between outside and inside for example. It's possible that causal connections between events somehow carry or facilitate acausal connections. See: C.G. Jung, 1960/2010, p.99

Chapter 10

[51] The mind/body organism can be subject to many and varied stresses. These stresses can have acute, sub-acute or chronic unbalancing effects in the susceptible organism. Such stress factors may be psychological, emotional, social, climatic, environmental, foods, electromagnetic, infectious, to name some of the most obvious. Samuel Hahnemann, the founder of homeopathy, classed all such unbalancing effects as "morbific influences". Morbific influences have a physical expression and effect but are not primarily physical in origin. They may be more like information fields or morphic fields as already discussed in chapters 4 and 5.

Chapter 11

[52] See the works of Freud and Jung. For an anthology of Jung's writing on dreams taken from Jung's Collected Works see: C.G. Jung, 1985, *Dreams*, Ark. Freud's *Interpretation of Dreams* was published in 1900.

[53] Rupert Sheldrake, 2012, *The Science Delusion*, Coronet, p.251

[54] Rupert Sheldrake, op. cit.

[55] For a lexicon of Jung's terminology (including *symbol*), see:
https://jungpage.org/learn/jung-lexicon

[56] Rupert Sheldrake, op. cit., pp.140-1

Chapter 12

[57] *The Gospel according to John*, 1,14, *Holy Bible*, King James version

[58] On the Christian and Alchemical understanding of redemption, see:

C.G. Jung, 1968, *Psychology and Alchemy* (Collected works, volume 12), Routledge and Kegan Paul, pp.306-316

[59] On the origins of these conflicts in the development of the human individual and of the human species, see: Erich Neumann, 1970, *The Origins and History of Consciousness*, Princeton University Press

[60] Namkhai Norbu (compiled and ed. John Shane), 1986, *The Crystal and the Way of Light: Sutra, Tantra and Dzogchen*, Routledge and Kegan Paul

[61] *The Gospel according to Matthew*, 17, 2, *Holy Bible*, King James version

Chapter 13

[62] See note 47.

[63] Quantum biology, which has been around since the pioneering days of quantum mechanics but is only now starting to be taken seriously by scientists, is considering the role of quantum laws operating at higher levels of complexity in nature. It's possible that in this area of research the theory of morphic resonance will be integrated with the known facts of quantum entanglement and coherence. See: World Science Festival, 'Quantum Biology: The Hidden Nature of Nature', YouTube, 17th Sept. 2015

[64] *The Book of Genesis*, 1, 2, *Holy Bible*, King James version

Chapter 14

[65] Julian Carlyon, op. cit., chapters 2 and 6

[66] For example, Katya Bloom, Margit Galanter and Sandra Reeve (eds), 2014, *Embodied Lives: Reflections on the Influence of Suprapto Suryodarmo and Amerta Movement*, Triarchy Press. See also: www.moveintolife.com

Chapter 15

[67] For modern science, absolute empty space isn't empty either: "According to present-day understanding of what is called the vacuum state or the quantum vacuum, it is 'by no means a simple empty space'. According to quantum mechanics, the vacuum state is not truly empty but instead contains fleeting electromagnetic waves and particles that pop into and out of existence." *Quantum vacuum state*, Wikipedia

[68] *The Essential Rumi*, 1997, trans. Coleman Barks, with J. Moyne, A.J. Arberry, R. Nicholson, Castle Books, p.36

Chapter 16

[69] There are many versions of the tarot pack. For the depiction of The Tower, see especially the *Rider-Waite* pack, originally published by William Rider.

Chapter 17

[70] In January 2013 Rupert Sheldrake gave a talk at TEDx (TED talks), entitled 'The Science Delusion'. The theme for the night was 'Visions for Transition: Challenging existing paradigms and redefining values (for a more beautiful world)'. In response to protests, the talk was taken out of circulation by TED, relegated to a corner of their website and stamped with a warning label. TEDx claimed, on the advice of their unnamed scientific advisory board, that Sheldrake's talk crossed the line into pseudoscience, contained serious factual errors and made many misleading statements. See https://blog.ted.com/graham-hancock-and-rupert-sheldrake-a-fresh-take/ where TEDx state their reasons for removing the talk, and also placed the video of the talk. At https://www.sheldrake.org/reactions/tedx-whitechapel-the-banned-talk there is more from Sheldrake himself.

[71] Ken Wilber has produced comprehensive meta studies mapping the common themes that emerge from the many different studies of the development of human consciousness. When looking at general stages of development seen in the species (rather than stages of individual development) he has drawn especially on the work of philosopher Jean Gebser. Gebser proposed an outline of human development, saying that we've passed through the archaic, magic and mythic stages of development, and are now in the mental/rational. The stages that emerge from and go beyond the rational – stages that are characterised by a more pluralistic view of the world and greater integration in human consciousness – are still in their infancy.

Wilber, building on Gebser's map, proposes the following stages of development of human consciousness: Archaic – Magic – Mythic – Rational – Pluralistic – Integral. See:

Ken Wilber, 1995, *Sex, Ecology, Spirituality*, Shambhala
Ken Wilber, 1996, *A Brief History of Everything*, Newleaf

[72] Classic scholarly sources on comparative mythology and ethnology include the work of C.G. Jung, Joseph Campbell and Mircea Eliade.

[73] For more on levels of development and the necessity to "transcend and include", see the works of Ken Wilber cited in note 71. See also, Julian Carlyon, op. cit, chapter 3

[74] Julian Carlyon, op cit., chapter 6

[75] For Jung's term *psychoid* see: www.carljungdepthpsychologysite.blog (search *psychoid*)

[76] See note 14

[77] C.G. Jung, 1960/2010 *Synchronicity: An acausal connecting principle*, Princeton University Press, pp.98-9

Index

Acknowledgements

For valued support and helpful comments on the manuscript I want to thank Sandra Reeve, Misha Norland, Mani Norland, Amanda Norland, David Friese-Greene, Wyn Rainbow and Lucy Lidell.

I also want to especially thank Andrew Carey for his continued support, guidance and hard work in the preparation of the manuscript.

About the Author

Julian Carlyon has been a practitioner and student of homeopathy for over 40 years. In that time, as well as teaching, he has studied with many of the world's leading homeopaths.

In the 1980s he trained in Jungian- based transpersonal psychology with British transpersonal psychology pioneers, Barbara Somers and Ian Gordon-Brown.

In the last 12 years Julian has also been a student of free movement practice based on the Amerta movement teaching of Suprapto Suryodarmo and Sandra Reeve. He is currently a student of the Diamond Approach based on the teachings of A.H. Almaas.

Julian is a father and grandfather and lives in Stroud, Gloucestershire in the UK.

www.sevenawareness.com

About Triarchy Press

Triarchy Press is an independent publisher of books that bring a wider, systemic or contextual approach to many different areas of life, including:

- Government, Education, Health and other public services
- Ecology, Sustainability and Regenerative Cultures
- Leading and Managing Organizations
- The Money System
- Psychotherapy and Arts and other Expressive Therapies
- Walking, Psychogeography and Mythogeography
- Movement and Somatics
- Innovation
- The Future and Future Studies

For topics and titles referenced by the author, see:

www.triarchypress.net/movement